WJEC GCSE
Hospitality & Catering

Lesley Woods • Scott Reynard

www.heinemann.co.uk
✓ Free online support
✓ Useful weblinks
✓ 24 hour online ordering

0845 630 44 44

WJEC
CBAC

Heinemann
Part of Pearson

Heinemann Education is an imprint of Pearson Education Limited, a company incorporated in England and Wales, having its registered office at Edinburgh Gate, Harlow, Essex, CM20 2JE. Registered company number: 872828

www.heinemann.co.uk

Heinemann is a registered trademark of Pearson Education Limited

Text © Pearson Education Ltd, 2009

First published 2009

12 11 10 09
10 9 8 7 6 5 4 3 2 1

British Library Cataloguing in Publication Data
A catalogue record for this book is available from the British Library.

ISBN 978 0 435501 02 0

Typeset by 𝓣 Tek-Art, Crawley Down, West Sussex
Original illustrations © Pearson Education Ltd, 2009
Cover photo/illustration © Masterfile
Printed in Italy by Rotolito

Websites
The websites used in this book were correct and up-to-date at the time of publication. It is essential for tutors to preview each website before using it in class so as to ensure that the URL is still accurate, relevant and appropriate. We suggest that tutors bookmark useful websites and consider enabling students to access them through the school/ college intranet.

Endorsement
This material has been endorsed by WJEC and offers high quality support for the delivery of WJEC qualifications. While this material has been through a WJEC quality assurance process, all responsibility for the content remains with the publisher.

Contents

Introduction

Welcome to GCSE Hospitality and Catering for WJEC. This book has been written specifically to support you during your WJEC GCSE in Catering, Hospitality or Hospitality and Catering.

This book can be used to support you during the following courses:
- Single GCSE in Catering
- Single GCSE in Hospitality
- Double GCSE in Hospitality and Catering

A lot of the information in the book can also be used to support other courses in hospitality.

The Hospitality and Catering Industry

The hospitality and catering industry is huge with a wide variety of establishments to work in and over a hundred jobs to choose from. Often people think of the hospitality industry as just hotels and restaurants and the jobs as being just chefs and waiting on staff. However, there is a lot more to the industry than this. This book will help you to develop a wider understanding of the industry.

The course

A course in Hospitality and Catering offers you a unique opportunity in the curriculum to develop your knowledge and extend your skills within hospitality and catering in a vocational context. It will provide opportunities for you to develop transferable skills such as customer service skills and a range of key functional skills, for example using maths in the context of portion control. It will give you the capacity to work both independently and within a team and also develop your creativity, imagination and innovative thinking.

The GCSE course is a suitable qualification for anyone who wants a broad background in this area. It will offer valuable preparation when you enter the world of work but also if you wish to progress to further education.

The course also encourages the investigation and study of hospitality and catering in a variety of contexts. In these contexts you are given opportunities to acquire competence, capability and critical skills through the creation, implementation, use and evaluation of a range of resources.

GCSE Catering, Hospitality and Hospitality and Catering requires learners to demonstrate knowledge and understanding of:

- the industry – accommodation, food and beverage, front-of-house
- the types of products and services provided
- a range of customer groups
- job roles, career opportunities and relevant training
- appropriate forms of communication within the industry
- the importance of record-keeping
- the range of equipment used in the hospitality and catering industry.

The book has used the above themes as a structure for the units and chapters for the content. This has been done to support your understanding of the course. Recipes in the book are similarly designed to challenge you in longer lessons, and so really help to develop your catering skills.

Assessment

The GCSE course uses a range of assessment techniques, including external exams and controlled practical tasks. These different techniques assess your ability to:

- Recall, select and communicate your knowledge and understanding of a range of contexts.
- Apply skills, knowledge and understanding in a variety of contexts and in planning and carrying out investigations and tasks.
- Analyse and evaluate information, sources and evidence, make reasoned judgements and present conclusions.

Throughout the book there is a large amount of support given to you both for preparing for exams and for the controlled practical tasks.

At the end of each chapter there is an Exam Café section. Exam Café can be used when revising and preparing for exams. It could be used in revision classes. In this feature there are a number of useful resources which will help you organise your revision such as exam checklists, practise exam questions, assess sample mark schemes and locate extra resources to stretch yourself. Exmainer tips also appear throughout the book.

Chapters 12 and 13 cover the practical assessments of the course, and give detailed advice and guidance on investigating, planning, carrying out and evaluating the task.

Features of the book

The book is structured in a user friendly way with several features to support you during the course. These features appear throughout the topics in this book.

CASE STUDY

These are real life examples of the information given in the topic. They include a question that links the contents of the case study to that of the topic.

TRY THIS

These are suggested practical activities that will help you to develop your knowledge and understanding of different topics.

ACTIVITY

This is an extended question based around the content of the topic that suggests ways in which you can develop and extend your knowledge and understanding in a theoretical way.

FIND OUT

These are activities that use Internet links and other means of research to help you develop your knowledge and understanding.

CHECK YOUR KNOWLEDGE

At the end of each spread there are three questions that check that you have understood the content on these two pages. These act as a plenary feature for the contents of that spread.

Acknowledgements

Scott Reynard wishes to thank Elizabeth Stewart for her invaluable contribution to his chapters.

The authors and publisher wish to thank the following for their kind permission to reproduce material:

The AA – page 147
The Ritz Hotel – page 24
St. Columba Hotel, Argyll – page 64
TGI Fridays – page 24

Crown Copyright material is reproduced with the permission of the controller of HMSO – page 44, 85

Every effort has been made to contact copyright holders of material reproduced in this book. Any omissions will be rectified in subsequent printings if notice is given to the publishers.

The authors and publisher wish to thank the following for their kind permission to reproduce photos:

Abraham Nowitz/Corbis – page 91
Alex Segre/Alamy – page 94
Alexander Iotzov/Shutterstock – page 84 [parsnip]
Aznym Adam/Shutterstock – page 84 [carrot]
Brendan Howard/Shutterstock – page 12
Carlos Davilla/Alamy – page 17
Claire Dunn/Alamy – page 2 [restaurant]
Cuboimages sri/Alamy – page 164
Dallas Events/Shutterstock – page 116
Design Pics Ltd/Alamy – page 165
The Dorchester – page 30 [bottom]
Food Drink and Diet/Mark Sykes/Alamy – page 86
Grafica/Shutterstock – page 89
Jennifer Stone/Shutterstock – page 16
Iofoto/Shutterstock – page 93
iStockphoto/Heiko Etzrodt – page 30 [top]
Jiri Vaclavek/Shutterstock – page 109 [oils]
Kate Mitchell/zefa/Corbis – page 9
Kwest/Shutterstock – page 10
Mike Flippo/Shutterstock – page 54
Mircea Bezerghenu/Shutterstock – page 109 [pulses]
Monkey Business Images/Shutterstock – page 107
Nathan Benn – page 87
Niderlander/Shutterstock – page 84 [fats]
Norman Chan/Shutterstock – page 59
Paul Cowan/Shutterstock – page 101
Pearson Education Ltd/Ben Nicholson – page 154 [both]
Pearson Education Ltd/Jules Selmes – page 13, 49
Pearson Education Ltd/Rob Judges – page 55, 67 [all], 96 [right]
Pearson Education Ltd/Mark Bassett – page 58
Peter Jones/Alamy – page 183
Photos.com/Jupiterimages – page 84 [chickpeas]
Photodisc/Cole Publishing Group/Michael Lamotte – page 56
Photodisc/Photolink – pages 110, 168
Photodisc/Steve Mason – page 76
Photofusion Picture Library/Alamy – page 11
Punchstock/Upper cut images – page 128
Rohit Seth/Shutterstock – page 92
Shenval/Alamy – page 2 [van]
Stephen Coburn/Shutterstock – page 28
Svry/Shutterstock – page 95
Terence Mendoza/Shutterstock – page 102
Ultimathule/Shutterstock – page 84 [bread]
-V-/Shutterstock – page 25
VR Photos/Shutterstock – page 73
Zsolt Nyulaszi/Shutterstock – page 78
ZTS/Shutterstock – page 96 [left]

THE UK HOSPITALITY INDUSTRY

1.1 The structure of the hospitality industry

The hospitality industry in the UK is a broad and varied industry ranging from single-person organisations to worldwide corporations. People do a total of more than 80 different jobs in the industry.

Seven sub-industries

The following seven sub-industries broadly define the hospitality industry:

These different industries will be looked at further in later chapters in this book.

Different-sized operations in the industry

Sally has her own burger van. She runs it on her own. She buys and cooks all the food and cleans the van at the end of the day.

Adil works for McDonald's as a manager. He is responsible for the daily running of the outlet and has many jobs, such as organising staff training, quality control and customer complaints.

Around 80 per cent of hospitality operations employ less than five people. This means that hospitality is a great industry for people who want to set up their own business – whatever it might be, as well as for people who want to progress their career in a multinational corporation.

These outlets both serve the same thing but are very different businesses

Different customers

Not everyone wants the same type of service or food. The industry has to identify people's different needs and offer suitable services and food to match those needs.

Some people want a cheap room – just somewhere to 'put their head down'. A hostel is ideal for this.

Some people want luxury – more than they'd have in their own home. They want a TV with 20 channels and home movies, a bar with room service, lots of 'smellies' to use in the bathroom and a robe and slippers.

Some people want to dress up and go to a casino, have a three-course meal and then, while gambling, have drinks brought to them by waiters. Other people want to go to their local bingo hall, have a snack and spend a few hours gambling, with a trip to the bar in between games.

More about the structure of the industry

The industry can also be divided in different ways:

Commercial or service sector

Is hospitality the main purpose of the industry? Is it the reason for the industry being there? Then it is a commercial operation. Or, is it there just because a lot of people stay, study or work there (such as a hospital)? In this case, it is a service operation.

Profit-making or working within a budget

Most hospitality operations need to make a profit but some don't, they just need to keep to a specific budget. For example, a lot of school canteens have a budget of 75p food cost per meal per day. In some workplaces, the canteen works to a budget but the prices are then reduced. A cheap lunch is an incentive to work there – a perk of the job.

Restricted customers or open to the general public

Most hospitality operations can sell to anyone but some are restricted to selling to a small part of the public: customers who are, for example, on the cross-channel ferry or on a train.

ACTIVITY

Compare a fast food restaurant you have visited with a pub restaurant (or other restaurant you might have visited such as an Indian or Italian restaurant).

Compare the differences under the headings of 'choice of menu', 'type of service', 'time taken to have the meal', 'healthy food' and 'music and décor'.

ACTIVITY

1 Add to the table below so that you have included all sectors of the industry you can think of.

2 Explain why the operations working to a budget do not have to make a profit.

CHECK YOUR KNOWLEDGE

1 What are the 7 sub industries of the hospitality industry?

2 Why do some establishments have a restricted number of customers?

3 List four different types of customers that might book into a hotel.

Commercial	Service	Profit making	Working to a budget	General public	Restricted customers
• Hotels • Hostels • Contract caterers, such as events	• Tourist attractions • Hospitals • Prisons • Colleges • Workplace including armed forces catering	• Most!	• Prison • Care home catering • NB: Workplace is often also subsidised. • Some organisations are a charity, e.g. YMCA	• Hotels	• Train, cruise and ferry catering • Tourist attractions • Casinos

1.2 Hospitality's contribution to the UK economy

The hospitality industry makes a major contribution to the UK economy and employs a large percentage of people. In some parts of the UK, the industry is the main source of income and employment.

KEY TERM

Turnover: the total amount of money passing through a business.

Hospitality's importance as a sector

In the UK, there are over 180,000 hospitality and leisure establishments and these employ more than 2 million people. That's about 7 per cent of the UK workforce.

Turnover

The hospitality industry's **turnover** in 2006 was £65 billion, compared to £21 billion in education and £5 billion in agriculture and fishing.

- Nearly half a million people are employed in restaurants.
- 400,000 work in the **service sector** (e.g. hospitals) of the industry.
- In this sector, two thirds of the workers are women.
- The same number of men and women work in restaurants.
- Overall, the industry employs a young workforce with over a third of staff being under 25.
- Restaurants in particular have a very young workforce.
- In the service sector, most workers are aged 35 to 55.

Turnover of different industry sectors.

Number of establishments

From 1995 to 2005, the number of restaurants grew from 46,000 to 63,000. At the same time, the number of hotels decreased from 12,500 to 10,000. The number of pubs increased from 46,000 to 49,000 and the number of hostels increased by 300 per cent – from 50 to 150!

Food and drink

By far the most number of meals sold is in the quick service sector. However, the revenue received is not much more than that received by hotels and restaurants.

KEY TERM

Service sector: part of the industry or business which deals with the marketing and selling of services rather than physical goods.

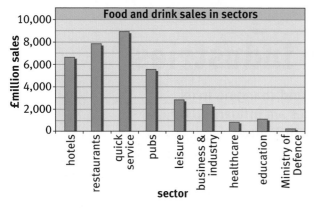

Food and drinks sales per sector

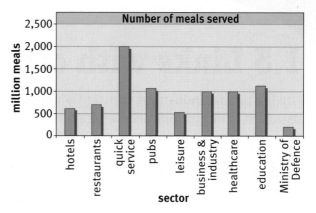

Number of meals served

Regional differences

About 7 per cent of the UK workforce is employed by the hospitality industry. Hospitality income is 2.5 per cent of the UK's total income. In some parts of the UK, however, the hospitality industry is far more important than these figures suggest.

CASE STUDY

The Isles of Scilly

Tourism is estimated to account for 85 per cent of the islands' income and 63 per cent of employment.

Most hospitality businesses, except for a few hotels, are small enterprises employing fewer than four people. Many are family run.

Because of the seasonality of tourism, many jobs are seasonal and part-time as work cannot be guaranteed throughout the year. Some islanders take up other temporary jobs 'out of season' to make up for this. Many seasonal workers are brought to the island just for summer.

The Isle of Wight

The Isle of Wight has a workforce of just under 50,000 people. Twenty-five per cent of these work in the hospitality industry. Two and a half million people visit the island for day trips and longer holidays. Hospitality and tourism is therefore an important part of the economy.

The city of Preston

In the north-west region of England over 200,000 people (6 per cent of the regional workforce) are employed in the hospitality and tourism industry. That is just below the national average, despite the popular resort of Blackpool being part of the region.

In the city of Preston, over 5,000 people are employed in the industry. More important is the 30 per cent increase in employment in this industry over the past 10 years. For some sectors, such as restaurants and cafés, this is closer to a 50 per cent increase.

- If the percentage of people taking holidays in this country fell by 20 per cent, because of the poor weather for several summers, what would the effect be on each of these areas?

ACTIVITY

1 Discuss why the revenue received by the quick service sector is not much more than received by hotels and restaurants.

2 Comment on the difference in the number of establishments mentioned and why this might be.

3 Look at the importance of the industry compared to other industries – what surprised you about these statistics?

FIND OUT

How important is the hospitality industry to your local area? How many people are employed by the industry and how much income does it generate?

CHECK YOUR KNOWLEDGE

1 What percentage of the workforce is employed by the hospitality industry?

2 How many people are employed in the restaurant sector?

3 What sectors had a reduction in establishments from 1995 to 2005?

4 What percentage of the population are employed by the hospitality sector in a) The Isle of Wight b) The Isles of Scilly?

1.3 Links with other industries

The hospitality industry is constantly developing and changing in its structure, client groups and services. These changes are influenced by other industries but the industry itself also has an influence.

The history of the hospitality industry

The timeline gives you examples of how the hospitality industry has developed.

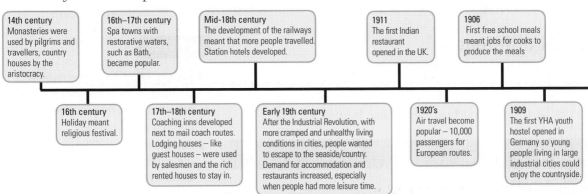

14th century
Monasteries were used by pilgrims and travellers, country houses by the aristocracy.

16th–17th century
Spa towns with restorative waters, such as Bath, became popular.

Mid-18th century
The development of the railways meant that more people travelled. Station hotels developed.

1911
The first Indian restaurant opened in the UK.

1906
First free school meals meant jobs for cooks to produce the meals

16th century
Holiday meant religious festival.

17th–18th century
Coaching inns developed next to mail coach routes. Lodging houses – like guest houses – were used by salesmen and the rich rented houses to stay in.

Early 19th century
After the Industrial Revolution, with more cramped and unhealthy living conditions in cities, people wanted to escape to the seaside/country. Demand for accommodation and restaurants increased, especially when people had more leisure time.

1920's
Air travel become popular – 10,000 passengers for European routes.

1909
The first YHA youth hostel opened in Germany so young people living in large industrial cities could enjoy the countryside.

You can see that the industry has changed because of the development of other industries. Manufacturing meant people needed to get away on holiday from cities. Railways and airplanes meant easier and cheaper travel. The way businesses developed from small to national and, often, multinational companies meant that more people travelled on business.

The hospitality industry 'feeds' off other industries, but other industries feed off hospitality operations too.

How hospitality is linked to leisure, travel and tourism

Holidays

The hospitality industry 'feeds' off leisure, travel and tourism because, as more people have disposable income to spend and more free time, the demand for holiday destinations increases.

Travel

More and more facilities are needed along and around the travel routes that people use to get to these destinations.

Leisure

The wider leisure industry, such as participating in or watching sport or going to the theatre, also increases the need for hospitality facilities.

Industry

Changes in manufacturing and industry also create demand for the hospitality industry. Many industrial organisations have increased in size and many national companies are being taken over by multinational corporations. This means that the demand for accommodation and meeting rooms increases.

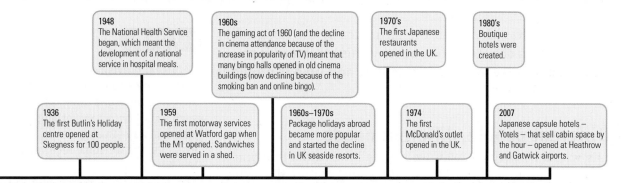

1948
The National Health Service began, which meant the development of a national service in hospital meals.

1960s
The gaming act of 1960 (and the decline in cinema attendance because of the increase in popularity of TV) meant that many bingo halls opened in old cinema buildings (now declining because of the smoking ban and online bingo).

1970's
The first Japanese restaurants opened in the UK.

1980's
Boutique hotels were created.

1936
The first Butlin's Holiday centre opened at Skegness for 100 people.

1959
The first motorway services opened at Watford gap when the M1 opened. Sandwiches were served in a shed.

1960s–1970s
Package holidays abroad became more popular and started the decline in UK seaside resorts.

1974
The first McDonald's outlet opened in the UK.

2007
Japanese capsule hotels – Yotels – that sell cabin space by the hour – opened at Heathrow and Gatwick airports.

How hospitality creates jobs and income for other industries

The simple opening of a fish and chip shop will support other industries:
- Local fish and potato suppliers get more business – and take on more staff.
- Local food packaging suppliers get more business.
- Maintenance company for deep-fat fryers get another contract – which means more jobs.

If a 4-star, 200-bed hotel with a wide range of facilities opens, the impact and support is even greater:
- The swimming pool needs two lifeguards.
- The spa needs four beauty therapists and two hairdressers.
- The hotel has a contract with a local laundry company to clean its bedding and towels – two jobs created.
- The hotel has a continuous refurbishment programme that employs two decorators full- time.
- Demand for food and drink supplies helps many local companies. For example, the hotel want to source ingredients locally, so the poultry farm increases its flock and employs another egg packer.

How jobs in hospitality support the local economy

As an example, the kitchen in the hotel above employs five full-time chefs and five kitchen porters. Their total monthly wages are £12,000 – money to spend in the local economy.

Three of the chefs moved to the area for their jobs. They bought new cars from two local car dealers. One chef has two children at the local school. Another bought a small house that he is extending using a local builder. Three of the workers spend a quarter of their wages in the local pub.

FIND OUT

Research the history of a particular sector of the industry, for example, Lyons tea rooms.

CHECK YOUR KNOWLEDGE

1 Why did the Industrial Revolution mean a bigger demand for holiday accommodation?

2 What is the connection between the development of the airplane and an increase in hospitality facilities?

3 How would a new hotel in a town affect the local fishmonger, the poultry farm up the road and the florist?

1.4 What services the industry provides and who it provides them for

Chapter 1.1 has identified the structure of the hospitality industry. This chapter looks at why this structure is so wide and diverse in what it provides and who it provides it for.

Different people, different needs

Life would be very boring if we were all the same. Imagine every restaurant in the whole country only selling the same dish every day of the year!

When I go out for a meal, I always have the steak and kidney pie with chips and chocolate ice cream. I don't expect to pay more than £10.

When I stay in a hotel, I have to have a choice of pillows and a dressing gown with slippers. Oh, and sky TV with all the sport channels. Price? It doesn't matter.

Wouldn't it be boring if we all wanted the same thing?

Services

The industry needs to provide various services for the different individuals that exist in the world.

The industry is wide and diverse. Different types of bedroom accommodation are available, from shared bunk bed rooms to luxury. Food ranges from the sandwich on a train journey to an eight-course gourmet taster meal at a Michelin-star restaurant. Drink ranges from a paper cup of coffee at an airport to a cocktail served by a skilled **mixologist**.

Some establishments target a distinct client and service. Others offer a wider range of services to several client groups.

Clients

People's needs don't stay the same. Needs change depending on whether people are on a business or leisure trip and whether they are on their own or in a group. Someone on their own will want a quick meal at a table on their own. Groups prefer round tables for better conversation. How does a restaurant cater for both types of client?

Let's have a celebration!

A celebration or party means different things to people at times of life so different establishments and services are needed. The following table shows some of the needs of service users.

KEY TERM

Client group: a particular type of customer (leisure or business customers, individuals or groups, different ages).

ACTIVITY

Study a local hospitality establishment. Identify the different services it offers and the different client groups it targets.

Age	Needs	Food implications	Facilities	Services
5-year-old	Lots of short activities Short attention span	Easy to eat food on the move Finger food?	A big room – could be anywhere – a village hall (will need caterers) or a hotel	An entertainer or organised games
10-year-old boy	Activities to use up energy Food to feed the fussiest person	Burgers or sandwiches	In a leisure centre so they can swim, play football, rock climb Or a specialist leisure organisation such as Go ape (high wire assault courses) Bowling alleys or a cinema	Lifeguard or sports instructor Specialist clothing Other leisure facilities
16-year-old teenager	Good dancing Invite loads of friends	Not important? Snack food only but filling food for growing people!	The right ambience created Perhaps a village hall or local night club/hotel function room	A good DJ with the right music and a good sound and lighting system
Young couple	Romantic	Themed food such as heart-shaped and aphrodisiac properties, such as asparagus	An intimate restaurant	Light entertainment such as a live pianist or guitarist
50-year-olds	Nostalgia – reliving their youth?	Possibly themed nostalgia food buffet style for socialising?	A certain standard of décor Room to dance	A specialist DJ for 80's or 70's music
80-year-old	Mobility – sitting down Not too tiring – middle of the day	Traditional food – a sit down 3-course meal	Traditional setting – not too noisy	A high standard of service – possibly a tea dance band

ACTIVITY

Plan a Christmas party for a group of thirty 7-year-old children and a group of thirty 70-year-old adults. Plan the menu and entertainment. Compare the differences in the food offered and how it will be served, as well as the entertainment.

CHECK YOUR KNOWLEDGE

1 Identify three specific client groups that might book into a restaurant.
2 Explain what type of client will book a hostel in a city.
3 Identify the type of event a 100-year-old lady might want to celebrate her birthday.

1.5 Accommodation facilities

The industry provides a range of accommodation services. Accommodation doesn't just mean bedrooms. It also means public areas such as function and conference rooms. These rooms have the same day-to-day needs as bedrooms, they need to be serviced in the same way: cleaned and set up for new customers – tea, coffee and snacks need replenishing, as well as toiletries or stationery.

Chains such as Hilton Hotels, have become major players in the hotel market

Sub-industry

The provision of accommodation facilities is a very important part of the industry and covers 3 out of the 7 sectors of the industry:

- hotels
- hospitality service
- membership clubs.

Hotels

The hotel sector is the largest sector, with a wide range of establishments from one- or two-bedded guest houses to 5-star luxury 300-bed hotels. This sector can be subdivided into:

- Hotels – 5-star to low cost, often serviced to a high level, with restaurants and bars. They include independent, owner run, large chains and independent consortia.
- Motels or lodges – usually near motorways or major roads and also now in or near airports. They provide basic low-cost accommodation and are semi-serviced (catering is nearby or trayed and packaged).
- Guesthouses or B&B's – usually just a few rooms, usually low cost but some are now boutique-style luxury guest houses. These are serviced with a limited range of catering – breakfast only.

FIND OUT

1 Accor, Hilton, Ramada, Holiday Inn, Premier Travel Inn, Radisson, Hotel du Vin, Jury Inn, Swallow and Marriott are some of the hotel chains in the UK. Research one of these and find out about their standards. Present your findings.

2 Many hotels are still individually owned. These hotels often join a **consortia** for marketing purposes. Find out about one consortia and the criteria needed to join. Go to www.slh.com or www.finesthotels.net

KEY TERMS

Consortium: an association or combination of hotels and investors, for the purpose of engaging in a joint venture, such as marketing and taking bookings.

Chain: hotel chains are branded hotels that offer uniform services and standards.

Hostels

This sector has only 450 establishments in the UK but is growing annually. Hostels range from YHA barns in fields to converted houses or purpose-built buildings, such as the YHA in Manchester. Most accommodation in hostels is bunk beds with four to six people on average in a room. Facilities are usually shared. Service is minimal, often clients make up their own beds. Catering is usually provided but sometimes kitchens are available.

Some hostels are situated in an area that can offer a range of outdoor activities, such as canoeing, rock climbing and walking.

Social accommodation

This could also be included under hostels or even small hotels. Social accommodation includes student housing – either self-catering or with meals, and residential homes for the elderly, which have a high level of service both for cleaning and the provision of meals.

Holiday centres

Holiday centres are often a mixture of serviced and self-catering accommodation. They range from low cost, such as a caravan park, to luxury, such as one with log cabins all with individual hot tubs. There are usually lots of leisure facilities in the centre, such as a swimming pool and play park.

Self-catering

This is unserviced accommodation where no catering is provided. This accommodation is usually let for full weeks, although the industry is becoming more flexible, with weekend and midweek lets available.

Aparthotels are increasing in popularity in cities, where daily lets are available.

Membership clubs

This sector has a very old tradition, especially in London. Some clubs do not provide accommodation but some do. The Union Jack Club for ex-servicemen is an example of one that runs like a hotel for its members.

Functions and conferences

These provide large-scale service, accommodating large numbers at any one time.

This type of accommodation can be in a purpose-built building with a wide range of rooms or part of a hotel's business. It can also be outside catering, such as a marquee in a garden or field.

There is a wide range of youth hostels available for use in this country

FIND OUT

1 Research the history of the YMCA or the YHA.

2 What type of holiday centres exist in your region?

CHECK YOUR KNOWLEDGE

1 Where will you find a motel?

2 Do most guesthouses serve dinner?

3 What are the advantages and disadvantages of using self-catering accommodation?

1.6 Eating and drinking establishments

Restaurants and bars are the two sectors in the industry that employ the most people – 850,000 out of a total 2 million workers – nearly half of all workers in the industry. These are also the sectors that have the most single establishments (rather than chains such as Starbucks): 120,000.

Restaurants and bars can in fact operate in all seven sub-sections of the industry. You will usually find a bar and restaurant in a casino and at least a fast-food outlet in a bingo hall. Restaurants exist in most tourist attractions and some form of catering is available in hostels.

Providing food and drink is as varied as the paper cup of coffee bought on the train to London to an eight-course gourmet taster meal at the Michelin-starred restaurant in the next town.

Restaurants

Like accommodation, eating establishments can also be subdivided into:

Café brands, such as Starbucks have helped make popular catering a growth industry

- **Takeaways:** (fish and chip shops, sandwich bars and ethnic outlets such as kebab shops) –*very quick service – often now delivered to your home.*
- **Fast-food outlets:** *in a specialised environment – especially the kitchen – very quick service.*
- **Popular catering:** (includes cafés and coffee shops including those found in retail stores). *Cafés focus on food, coffee shops on beverages.*
- **Mainstream catering:** ethnic and themed – *usually medium to high prices with good levels of service.*
- **Fine dining:** *high levels of skilled service both in the kitchen and front-of-house.*

Sometimes it is easy to compare two different types of eating establishments to recognise the different eating experience they provide:

Fast-food restaurant	Ethnic restaurant – e.g. Italian
Small choice on menu	Wide choice on menu
Cheap price	Medium price
Counter service from operators in a casual uniform	Waiters in smart uniform serve you at the table
Food is packaged – to keep warm	Food is well presented on the plate
Food is precooked and ready when ordered	A wait for freshly cooked dishes
Plastic seating. No music. Hard flooring. Plastic tables.	Music and carpet, comfortable seating and tablecloth.

So to generalise you could define eating establishments as:

Low cost   ←————————→   High cost

Small choice on menu ←————————→ Wide choice

Quick service of food ←————————→ Slow service of food (cooked to order)

Self-service   ←————————→ High level of service

Basic ambience   ←————————→ High level of ambience

Pubs and bars

Is the traditional pub a dying breed?

The traditional pub has a long history in the UK but around 36 a week close because of changes in society. They have particularly suffered from the effect of stricter enforcement of drink-driving laws and the smoking ban. So, for many years, pubs and bars have had to diversify to attract a wider or different client group. Some examples of this diversification are:

- **Sports bars:** with large-screen TV's showing live sport, especially football matches.
- **Cocktail bars:** with sophisticated décor and a cocktail menu. Often doormen enforce a dress code for customers, such as no trainers or jeans.
- **Wine bars:** a little like continental coffee bars. They offer a wider choice of drinks than the traditional pub, such as teas and coffees. This type of bar attracts a wider clientele, such as single women, because of the ambience created.
- **Family-friendly pubs:** with an outside playground and sometimes one inside. Food is particularly important for these pubs.

The pub and bar industry is a high profit-margin industry. The mark-up on drinks is often 200 per cent – the same as food, but there is no labour cost on preparing drinks! Wine bought in a supermarket costs from £3 – wine in a bar or restaurant costs from £10.

Cola bought in a supermarket costs 50p – cola bought in a bar costs £2.50.

1.7 Types of food service

One of the reasons that the restaurant industry is the largest sector is because it offers a wide range of experiences – in the food available but also in the service provided.

Food can be served in many ways. The type of service chosen depends on the following factors:

- the type of establishment or where it is
- the type of food or menu being served
- the cost of the meal or food
- the time available for the meal
- the type of customer
- the number of customers expected
- the availability of skilled serving staff.

The types of service can be divided into three main methods:

1 table: meals served to seated guests
2 counter: meals collected by guests
3 personal: delivered meals.

Each method can be subdivided:

Table

Method	Description	Comments
Plate	Pre-plated meals from the kitchen Can be a basic plated meal or decorated nouveau cuisine style	From cafés to luxury restaurants Good portion control methods Consistent presentation of food Relies more on skilled kitchen staff than the skill of serving staff Time consuming for kitchen Can be boring for staff who serve
Family	Dishes are put on the table where spoons are provided and customers serve themselves Suited to ethnic restaurants such as Indian, Chinese and Spanish tapas	Sociable Less portion control Easy and quick to serve Suits families with young children Needs big tables to fit all the dishes on
Silver	Food is served by the staff using spoon and fork. Full silver service is when all food is served in this way Semi-silver service is when the meat or fish is served plated and vegetables are served with a spoon and fork. This often happens for banquet service with large numbers of people	A more personal customer experience Can be a slow service Expensive Portion control may fluctuate Staff costs are high as it needs more serving staff
Guéridon	Food is served from a side table or trolley using a spoon and fork Sometimes dishes are assembled or cooked in front of the customer e.g. Steak Tartare, Steak Diane or crêpe Suzette	Very specialist, skilled service Individual attention Very high staff costs and menu costs A time consuming service

Counter

Method	Description	Comments
Cafeteria (free flow)	A single long display counter but can sometimes be multiple counters	Queuing is often required It can be fast so can produce a high turnover A simple, basic experience for customers There can be impulse buying from displays Low skill of serving staff
Buffet	Set up in a room usually along one table. It can be self-service or staff can serve customers. Carvery service is where joints of meat are carved in front of customers and plated	Creates a more informal function than plated or silver service meals It can be fast and simple It can be quite low cost depending on the type of food served Poor portion control Needs efficient clearing away of crockery
Fast food	Takeaway with eat-in area where customers collect food from one small counter	A quick simple method of service Can be a very high turnover of food Often a limited choice of menu Use of disposable packaging and utensils because of the type of food and service

Personal

Method	Description	Comments
Tray or trolley	An assembled meal provided or a choice of food and drink from a trolley	Available where needed Trays are used in airlines, hospitals and hotel rooms (room service) Trolleys are used in offices, airlines and trains
Vending	Sold from a machine	24-hour service if required Drinks, snacks and meals can be offered including hot meals
Home delivery	Delivered to house individually or on a round	Usually ethnic such as Italian, Indian and Chinese. Also 'Meals on Wheels'.

CASE STUDY

Japanese tepanyaki restaurants are an entertainment as well as an eating experience. Show chefs perform as they cook the food. Eight customers sit around one griddle while the chef cooks their orders. He juggles eggs and other ingredients and often throws bits of food into the customers' mouths!

- Go to YouTube.com or www.sapporo.co.uk to see tepanyaki chefs in action.

TRY THIS

1 Create a balanced airline meal that fits into the designated containers on a tray.
2 Learn how to make a Steak Diane or crêpe Suzette so that you could carry out Guéridon service with this dish.

CHECK YOUR KNOWLEDGE

1 What is semi-silver service and when is it often used?
2 What is the main advantage of a vending machine?
3 What is carvery service?

15

1.8 Contract catering, hospitality services and events

Hotels and restaurants – accommodation services and food and drink, are the two major sectors of the hospitality industry. The other major sectors are contract catering, hospitality services and events.

Contract catering and hospitality services

These overlap each other considerably.

- If the catering is managed in-house, it is a hospitality service.
- If it is outsourced to a catering or events firm, it is a contract food service.

Both sectors provide food and drink services within other organisations whose main focus is not hospitality.

It is often easier to ignore whether the service is in-house or outsourced and to divide these sectors into industrial catering and welfare catering.

Industrial catering

Industrial catering is any catering service carried out at a workplace. An estimated 50 per cent of the total meals served in the industry are served in this sector. The sector has shown rapid growth over the past 20 years. Half of all outlets are contracted out to a specialised firm, such as Sodexo or Aramark.

Companies started to set up staff restaurants in the nineteenth century as part of employers' attempts to look after the welfare of workers. So they are seen as an important part of the employment package. Restaurants are often subsidised by the employer.

A wide range of services can be provided in industrial catering as it includes catering for company directors to shopfloor workers.

Welfare catering

Welfare catering can be defined as the provision of meals for those unable to provide for themselves, either physically not being able to or having no time. This sector includes hospitals, schools, colleges, universities, prisons and social care, such as 'meals on wheels' and day centres.

In this sector, the catering operation is not there to make a profit but often works to a tight budget per meal or day. For example, in prisons the average food cost allocation per day in 2000 was £1.44. One of the key aims with this type of catering is to provide a nutritious balanced meal.

A vending machine can supply contract goods quickly and easily

CASE STUDY

The workers in a mechanical fittings factory in Cardiff have a vending machine available to them at all times which serves hot drinks and snacks.

- What catering facilities are there in a factory near you?

CASE STUDY

CGC Events based in Leeds operate all over the north of England. They run the Paris and Farnborough airshows and provide catering at most of the northern racecourses, such as Pontefract and Redcar. They also run private events, such as weddings and garden parties.

- Are there any similar operations to CGC events in your area?

Nutritional guidelines for school meals have recently been updated so that school canteens must offer oily fish once a week and only offer chips twice a week.

Nutrition is the key to many hospital meals. A dietician will oversee the production of some specialist diet meals, such as low potassium for renal (kidney) patients.

Every sector is different in how meals are produced and how meals are served:

- **Hospital catering:** large-scale with up to thousands of meals produced for patients, staff and visitors. Patient meals usually served on trays in a similar way to airline meals.
- **School meals:** usually cafeteria-style, from 50 primary pupils in a rural school to over a 1,000 meals in a large comprehensive.
- **Prison meals:** unique in that prisoners help to produce them. Some prisons have a farm or market garden and the produce is used for meals.

A plating and traying system used in hospitals

Events

The events sector is often called 'outside catering', as many events are carried out at different sites at different and irregular times of the year.

Events can range from a garden party for 20 people to catering for thousands at an air show or a Grand Prix.

Outside catering can be for a:

- **Contracted function:** the organisation is catering for a specific number of people and type of meal (very similar to banqueting).
- **Speculative function:** the organisation supplies food and drink for the public attending the event. The risk is high here. Bad weather can significantly affect numbers attending.

Two types of caterers

1 Non-specialist: Some outside catering is carried out by hotels and restaurants but this is often difficult to do well as it uses up the establishment's staff and equipment so that standards at the establishment are lowered.

2 Professional outside catering firms: Most events are carried out by these firms. They range from the sole trader (people running businesses on their own) for example a mobile ice-cream van, up to very large firms. On average, three quarters of outside caterers are sole traders, with 90 per cent of all operations employing less than 10 staff.

ACTIVITY

Compare the types of school or college meals your parents or grandparents ate with the type of meals offered today.

FIND OUT

1 Study your school or college catering system. What cost and nutritional restraints do they have?
2 What kind of special diets do hospitals have to cater for?

CHECK YOUR KNOWLEDGE

1 What is the difference between contract catering and hospitality services?
2 What is the difference between industrial and welfare catering?
3 What is unusual about prison catering?
4 What problems may a hotel face if it carries out a special event outside the hotel?

Exam preparation

Revision checklist

Which exam	Content	What to revise
HOS but an overview needed for CAT	The structure of the industry	You need to have a clear understanding of the breadth of the industry and how there are different sized operations as well as different reasons for operations.
HOS	The importance to the UK economy and links with other industries	You need to know the importance of each sector and how important hospitality is to certain areas of the UK. You also need to know how different industries feed off hospitality and how hospitality feeds off other industries.
Mostly HOS	Different services – different needs	You need to be aware that there is a wide range of clients with different needs, so there is a wide range of establishments and services to meet these needs.
HOS	Accommodation facilities	You need to be able to compare different facilities – the size and facilities they provide.
CAT but some for HOS	Eating and drinking facilities	You need to be able to compare different establishments. The type of menu, cost and ambience of them.
BOTH	Types of food service	You need to be able identify what type of service matches with what type of establishment.
BOTH	Contract Catering, Hospitality Services and Events	You need to understand about these types of hospitality services and how they are different to hotels and restaurants

Common mistakes

You need to know the technical terms for different types of establishments such as hotel and guest house or contract catering. You also need to know, for example, what plate, silver and guéridon service is. If you don't know these terms and what they mean, you cannot answer questions about them.

So, make sure that you learn definitions.

Activities

Practice comparing different types of establishments such as a hotel and guesthouse, a hostel and a four-star hotel or a fast-food restaurant and a fine dining restaurant. Think about the different types of hospitality establishments you have visited in your life to help you.

Summarising content

Create a spider diagram of all the different types of establishments. Try to add as much detail about each type as you can.

Exam preparation

Sample question

1 Many hotels are now providing conference facilities.
   a Suggest two groups that may use these facilities. (2 marks)
   b Name three items a group may need during the conference. (3 marks)
   c Some delegates (people attending) may require accommodation.
   d State two advantages to the hotel and two advantages to the delegate. (4 marks)

Sample answer

a business groups
  training groups

b pens, paper, tea
  and coffee.

c more customers using the
  rooms more money

d don't have to travel on
  the day can use the facilities

Sample question

2 There is a range of food outlets within the hospitality and catering industry. Describe the main features of each of the following:

a	a fast-food outlet	(4 marks)
b	a café	(4 marks)
c	an exclusive restaurant	(4 marks)

Sample answer

a Lots of teenagers use these. The menu is fairly unhealthy and usually just burgers or chicken. You buy the food from a counter and can eat in or out. You usually eat with your fingers

b This serves breakfast as well and different meals. Lots of older people go here for cups of tea. There are cafés in every town and village so they are very convenient to get to. Some cafés are self-service and some have waitress service.

c This has carpet and music and nice decorations. The waiters wear a uniform and serve food in a professional way. The menu has lots of different items on, such as starters, main courses and desserts. The food is expensive.

Planning and structuring an answer

All questions with four or more marks should be approached as if you are writing a mini essay. Planning should happen before writing the answer. These questions get full marks when answers are 'well written and detailed'. This means well-structured. A well-structured answer is like an essay and has an introduction and a conclusion (or end) to it. For the above question, this planning can simply be:

• Menu: limited, more, different courses
• People: teenagers, older people, all for special occasions
• Cost: cheap to expensive
• Service: quick and simple – hands, quite quick – waiter or self, slow but nice

This planning would allow for the comparisons between the outlets and a well-written detailed answer.

Chapter 2

JOB ROLES IN HOSPITALITY

2.1 Introduction to employment opportunities

There are over 100 different types of job in the hospitality industry. There are jobs as chefs, restaurant managers and receptionists, but also jobs such as mixologists, sommeliers, housekeepers, events co-ordinators, food and beverage managers and concierges.

The many job opportunities in the hospitality industry can be seen from the career map found at www.uksp.co.uk.

Jobs in the hospitality industry can be divided into the sectors they are available in, such as hotels or gambling, or identified by where they sit in the staff structure of an organisation. To put it simply, there are three levels of jobs:

Managers ⟷ Supervisors ⟷ Craft or operative staff

Managers

These are the people in charge of running an operation or a major part of the operation.

In a small 20-bed hotel, there might be only one manager. In a 300-bed hotel, there might be seven different departmental managers that include:

- Finance manager
- Conference and banqueting manager
- Reservations or sales manager
- Food and beverages manager
- Head chef
- Front-office manager
- Housekeeping manager

In this type of operation, there will also be a general manager who has overall responsibility for the business.

Managers have many responsibilities and, unlike supervisors and craft or operative staff, their jobs vary from day to day. Their job role includes:

- ensuring that all procedures are carried out, *such as how to welcome customers at reception*
- setting and monitoring standards of service and products, *such as how quickly people are served at breakfast*
- motivating and training staff, *such as induction training when staff join the organisation*
- helping to set budgets and monitor spending, *such as the maintenance budget for the building*
- preparing staff rotas including holiday rotas
- ensuring that the supervisors are doing their jobs
- dealing with complaints
- making sure that all the relevant legislation is followed
- ensuring that wages are paid and all goods are ordered.

FIND OUT

Visit several hospitality operations and draw diagrams of their staffing structure.

ACTIVITY

Describe the advantages of a traditional staff structure and what the advantages are of a flexible structure.

Supervisors

Supervisors carry out the day-to-day tasks needed to run the operation but also check that all the staff are carrying out their job properly. They help staff to do this and will also be involved in any training that staff need. Supervisors are the first people to deal with customer complaints. They also pass on information and instructions from managers.

Craft and operative Staff

Craft and operative staff are those whose main responsibility is to carry out the day-to-day tasks needed for an operation to run smoothly. Craft staff have specific practical skills, such as chefing, and will have trained for a number of years to gain their skill.

An organisation's structure

Some hospitality organisations have a traditional and formal job structure where everyone has a clearly defined role. These jobs are often divided into areas and sub areas:

Area 1: Food and drink service – 1 Food preparation, 2 Front of house.

Area 2: Accommodation operations – 1 Front office, 2 Housekeeping.

In other organisations, the structure is more flexible. Staff are expected to do several jobs across all these different areas.

General assistants might be asked to serve breakfast, clean the bedrooms and set up a conference room for a wedding. On another day, they might be asked to assist the housekeeper with the laundry, sweep up the leaves in the garden and then serve lunch.

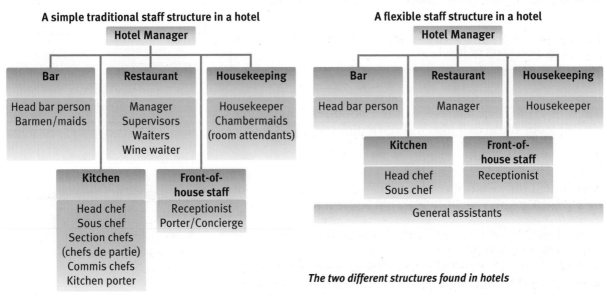

The two different structures found in hotels

2.2 Food and drink service jobs – food preparation

Food preparation jobs are the backstage roles of food and drink service. They include all types of chef's duties, kitchen assistant and kitchen porter duties. Below are adverts for two very different food preparation jobs.

Head chef

We require a head chef to manage the operation of the kitchen and food preparation.

You will have knowledge of relevant legislation, company policies and procedures, quality control, stock rotation, dietary requirements.

People management skills are needed.

You will:

- ensure that all dishes are prepared, cooked and presented to high standards, are of the highest quality and that regular temperature checks are carried out
- manage and be responsible for the whole process of stock ordering and stock taking
- effectively plan and co-ordinate team resources on shift
- lead, develop and motivate the kitchen team
- be able to identify training needs and coach individuals within the team as needed and oversee training of staff
- maintain the relevant documentation and ensure all wastage is recorded and actioned.

You must have 3 years experience in a similar role from a quality restaurant or hotel.

Kitchen porter

We have a great opportunity for an experienced kitchen porter with a friendly and warm attitude, who can work hard and respect the people he/she works with.

Your duties will include:

- washing-up
- cleaning cooking and service equipment
- cleaning and preparation of vegetables for Chef
- setting up and striking of tables and equipment for functions, and so on.

CASE STUDY

Neil Smith worked as a chef in hotels for 10 years. He is now the Catering Manager for a contract catering company providing food for customers at an educational activity centre in Bristol. 80% of customers are school children.

- What will be the difference in the food he now produces?

These two job roles have very different duties. The people carrying out these two jobs will have different skills and different training.

There is no formal training to be a kitchen porter. Often people will only earn the minimum wage. A one-day level 1 or 2 Food Hygiene certificate would be beneficial for the job.

A head chef is likely to have spent many years working in a kitchen and have formal training qualifications such as NVQ levels 1 to 4 completed over the years on day release or during in-house training.

Chef's skills

All chefs need the following skills when working with food:

- **organisational** – control of ingredients and timing
- **preparation** – weighing and measuring
- **cooking** – grilling, boiling, poaching
- **manipulative** – knife skills, decorating
- **presentation** – artistic, creative
- **personal** – pride in work, personal hygiene, teamwork.

A head chef will also need to be:

- **motivational** – leading other staff to aspire to produce quality work
- **organisational** – planning of menus and quantities of ingredients, forecasting demand and timing, organising equipment, staff and purchase of ingredients, control of staff, ingredients and time
- **creative** – creating menus with the right mix of flavour, texture and appearance.

The structure of a traditional kitchen brigade in a large restaurant or hotel shows the **career progression** that chefs can make in this sector.

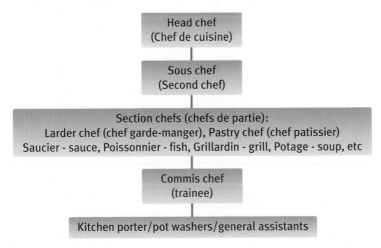

A traditional kitchen brigade

Some chefs choose to specialise, such as a pastry chef who makes all the desserts and bread, or a larder chef who is in charge of the cold room and prepares joints of meat as well as cold starters, and so on.

Not all jobs for chefs use this formal structure. Many operations only need one or two food preparation staff. Operations such as a school canteen or care home often have a head cook or chef and several kitchen assistants. A café at a tourist attraction might only require a kitchen assistant if cakes and scones are bought in from a supplier. Also, the skills of a chef in a bingo hall fast-food restaurant will be different to the skills required by a chef in a Michelin-starred restaurant.

2.3 Food and drink service jobs – front-of-house

Front-of-house food and drink service jobs are where staff interact with customers. They are roles such as waiters, restaurant managers and bartenders. They are also jobs such as sommeliers at the Ritz hotel in London and 'hosts' at TGI Friday's around the country.

Sommeliers are trained and knowledgeable wine professionals, usually working in fine restaurants who specialise in all aspects of wine service. They usually buy the wine, and control the storage of it. They are also responsible for the development of wine lists and are responsible overall for the delivery of wine service and training for the other restaurant staff. They work with the chef to pair and suggest wines that will best complement each menu item.

Hosts at TGI Friday's are the people who greet customers at the door and seat them at free tables. If there are no free tables, they keep the guest posted about the situation and keep them occupied with nibbles and chatter. On busy nights, there might be four hosts, whereas on other nights just one. Other people actually take orders and serve the food.

As you can see from these two job descriptions, a front-of-house worker needs to be:

- **knowledgeable** and enthusiastic about the drink and food they will serve
- **skilled** in how to serve this food and drink
- well presented and with good customer skills – in other words, they need good **personal skills**.

Training and qualifications

People who work in front-of-house jobs can also gain qualifications on day release, full-time college or university courses or through in-house training. These qualifications can be general, such as an NVQ Catering studies Front of House, which can be completed through day release or in-house, or specialist, such as WSET Level 3 Advanced Certificate in Wines and Spirits. This is a four-day course and involves a multiple-choice and written exam, as well as a practical test of blind-tasting a wine.

Knowledge of food and drink

Restaurant staff know how each dish has been made and which ingredients are included in the dish. This is often told to them by the chef at the beginning of service, but staff may also have the opportunity to taste the dishes for a deeper understanding.

Bartenders pride themselves in their knowledge of drinks and the different cocktails they can make. They will have tasted all the different types of drinks and have practiced making these cocktails. Wine waiters have an extensive knowledge of wine and have tasted a wide variety of different grape types.

Serving skills

Some restaurant staff will have the skill to serve Guéridon-style and cook dishes in front of customers. Other staff might carve a chicken or bone a fish in front of customers.

Generally, staff will know how to silver-serve and be able to stack several plates together when clearing a table.

In some bars, bartenders will pride themselves in their serving skills. They will be employed for their entertainment value: their ability to throw glassware, bottles and ingredients in the air as well as be able to free-pour the drink rather than measure the alcohol out.

Serving skills are sometimes as much of an attraction to customers as the venue

Personal skills

Any person who works in the hospitality industry and interacts with customers must have a high standard of personal appearance. They must be clean and tidy but must also show good posture and look as if they are enjoying their job – they must smile! They must also be friendly, know how to talk to customers in the correct way and have the confidence to ask them whether their meal is satisfactory.

2.4 Accommodation services – front office

Just like food and beverage service, accommodation service has a front-of-house operation and a backstage operation. The front-of-house is the reception area of a hotel or any other accommodation provider and is called the front office. Housekeeping is the backstage part of the operation.

Front office

This can sometimes be called reception but it is often a lot more than that. The front office:

- checks customers in and out

But it also:
- makes the original reservation (sometimes there is a separate sales office that does this)
- encourages guests to make a booking when they make an initial enquiry – sells the hotel
- provides guests with their first impression of the hotel
- communicates guests' needs to other departments – makes a restaurant booking, organises an extra pillow, and so on
- encourages guests to spend their money in other areas of the hotel, such as the restaurant
- plays a major part in making sure that guests are happy during their stay
- deals with guests' accounts so that all items, such as phone calls and bar bills, are paid for.

Communication and service

First impressions count!

How can I help you?

What do you want?

Hello Sir – did you have a good journey?

Hang on a minute!

These are some of the ways that a receptionist might speak to customers coming through the door at a hotel. Which ones would make people welcome and encourage them to return?

Saying the right things – being a good verbal communicator – is only one part of working in a front office. As with front-of-house in food and beverage service, personal appearance is very important. Workers need to look neat and tidy.

Body language is also important – a person's posture and mannerisms can create an impression of interest and alertness or one of indifference and reluctance to help.

RECEPTION

RECEPTION

Body language and presentation are vital in a customer facing role

Part of body language is eye contact and facial expression. A smile can go a long way in making people feel welcome and comfortable. This is **non-verbal communication**.

IT skills

Most booking systems and payment systems are now computerised. These are often specialised IT packages that can be particular to a specific hotel, hostel or group of accommodation operations. In-house training would be provided.

Front office jobs

The organisation of a front office varies depending on the type and size of the establishment.

In a motel that is a bedroom-only operation, the office will do all of the accounting and support duties, such as booking taxis and providing information about the area.

In a large hotel, there is likely to be a front desk and a back office, as well as a separate sales or reservations department.

In a large hotel, there is likely to be the following front-of-office staff:

A **front office manager** oversees the operation and carries out general management duties, such as training, dealing with complaints and organisation of staff.

A **receptionist** checks guests in and out, answers queries and liaises with other departments. In a large hotel, there will be a head receptionist or shift leader who controls and monitors the other receptionists.

A **concierge** is employed in very large hotels. This person is in charge of a team of porters and door staff. They help guests with:

- tickets and directions to local attractions, theatres and sports events
- restaurant reservations
- car hire, airline and train tickets
- any other special requests.

In most hotels, there is often just a **porter** who will do some of the above – the rest will be done by the receptionist. The main duty of a porter is to carry guests' luggage.

Often, porters support other departments in moving furniture around and helping to set up function rooms.

A **night porter** is often the only worker awake in a hotel overnight. He or she will answer the telephone and any queries from guests. Sometimes, night porters provide a restricted room service of snack food. They also often set up conference rooms for the following day.

KEY WORDS

Verbal communication: communication with words.

Non-verbal communication: communication in other ways than using words: body language, facial expression, and so on.

Through both these types of communication, staff need to be able to interact with customers and show a willingness to help the customer by putting their needs first. This is customer service and will be discussed further in chapter 10.

ACTIVITY

Carry out role-plays in groups, where different customers arrive at or are staying at a hotel and request different services from the staff. Make sure you all get a turn at playing the front-of-house staff. Then, discuss the performances of the staff.

CHECK YOUR KNOWLEDGE

1 What is the purpose of the front office?
2 Why is non-verbal communication so important?
3 What is the role of a receptionist?
4 What is the role of a porter?

2.5 Accommodation services – housekeeping

Housekeeping is the backstage part of the accommodation services operation. Most staff employed in the housekeeping department are involved in the practical cleaning and room servicing. Most of the jobs in this operation are room attendant jobs.

Room attendant

This is a very physically demanding job that includes many varied tasks. Typically, a room attendant is responsible for cleaning 15 rooms per shift. The actual amount of work depends on the size of the room and the number of beds. On average, you need between 15 and 30 minutes to do one room. A room attendant carries out the following physical tasks:

- making beds
- tidying rooms
- cleaning and polishing toilets, taps, sinks, bathtubs and mirrors
- washing floors
- removing stains and vacuuming.

Housekeeping services are vital for a successful business

Cleaning schedule

Room attendants usually follow a cleaning schedule or routine to make sure that the same standards are achieved. Most cleaning in a bedroom is carried out every day. A daily cleaning schedule for a hotel bedroom might be:

1 Open the windows to ventilate the room.
2 Empty waste bins (and ashtrays).
3 Flush the toilet and put in detergent.
4 Strip the bed – if the guest is leaving.
5 Clean and restock the hospitality tray – tea and coffee.
6 Remove all rubbish, dirty linen and dirty crockery.
7 Remake the bed.
8 Clean the bathroom including the floor.
9 Dust or damp-wipe the furniture – systematically from door to door so nothing is missed.
10 Spot-clean the walls, especially around the light fittings and doors.
11 Vacuum the carpet.
12 Replace the hotel stationery and literature.
13 Close the window.
14 Check all electrical fittings are working correctly – report any defects.
15 Check the room's overall appearance – straighten pictures and remove mirror smears.
16 Lock the door and report to housekeeper.

Room attendants will often then go on to clean public areas and corridors.

In some hotels, there are late-duty room attendants who go into the rooms in the early evening, turn down bedcovers, close curtains and switch on bedside lamps. They sometimes leave a chocolate on the pillow. This is usually in more expensive hotels and helps to make guests feel welcome when they return to their rooms.

Periodic cleaning and maintenance

There is extra cleaning that does not have to be done each day:

- There might be weekly upholstery cleaning done in rooms, with a set day for each room or floor of rooms.
- Bed-turning is carried out every one to two months in most accommodation operations, depending on occupancy.

Maintenance

In large operations, there is a permanent maintenance team that might consist of permanent painters and decorators, who systematically redecorate bedrooms and public areas. Maintenance staff might be on call 24-hours a day so that any faults can be sorted out immediately.

Managing accommodation operations

The housekeeper is the accommodation manager and carries out managerial jobs, just like in all of the other departments of an establishment. They will train staff, organise rotas, motivate staff and set standards. They will order cleaning materials as well as maintain the stock of linen and towels. They will check bedrooms once a room attendant has completed cleaning. They will also liaise with other departments, especially the front office, so that they are aware of when rooms can be occupied. This is now usually done using **ICT**.

Key issues in accommodation operations

Cleaning materials

The COSHH regulations are part of the Health and Safety at Work Act (see Chapter 4.4 for further information about this act). This regulation states that training must be given about use of chemicals. This is particularly important for workers in this sector. The training must include both use and storage of chemicals. This regulation is one reason why workers in this sector wear a uniform.

Environmental issues

The housekeeping section of a business can have a real influence on how environmentally friendly the establishment can be. Bed linen and towels in guest's rooms are changed frequently. This is expensive, so most hotels have introduced a towel reuse programme where guests leave their towels hanging if they wish to reuse them, on the floor if they want them washed.

Other ways to be more environmentally conscious are turning off lights and the television when rooms are unoccupied, and turning down the heating until guests arrive.

2.6 Conference and events jobs

For many hotels, functions such as conferences and banquets, are such an important part of their business that they employ special managers for each of this type of function.

A typical hotel conference room

Some operations specialise in the function business. Examples include conference centres and events organisers, or outside catering organisations that use a wide variety of facilities, including marquees and village halls, to run the event.

Sales and revenue manager

In large establishments, sales and operations are separated into different departments.

Sales departments look after the initial stages of a conference or banquet booking. Bookings are often just carried out over the phone or via email but some personal visits are also made by customers.

The Ballroom at the Dorchester Hotel. It can hold 1,000 people

From an initial phone call, an enquiry form is filled in with:
- the name of customer
- contact details
- type of function requested
- date of conference
- number of people
- room set up, for example, theatre, cabaret
- budget (amount of money to spend)
- facilities such as daylight or blackout.

The diary is checked and rates are discussed. These might be day-delegate rates that include room hire and food and drink, or might be broken down into separate parts including the cost of hiring a projector or the cost of a live band.

At this stage, a provisional booking can be made. Confirmation is requested within a certain time, when a booking contract is sent to the customer. It must then be signed and returned. The booking is then confirmed and a file created.

Conference and banqueting manager

This file is handed over to the operations department a few weeks before the event.

The manager of this department is the conference and banqueting manager. In large operations there might be a separate conference manager and a separate banqueting manager. Conferences are usually Monday to Friday and during the day. Banqueting is usually at the weekend and in the evenings.

When the conference manager receives a file about a conference, he or she rings the customer to check that none of the details have changed: for example, the number of guests might have altered. The information about the conference is also handed to the head chef and the food and beverage manager.

At the beginning of the day, the manager will make sure that each conference delegate has access to water and a pen and paper. The manager will also liaise with the conference leader for that day about break and lunch times and check that they have all the equipment they need.

The room is serviced – replenished with fresh water and teas and coffees, regularly during the day. A successfully organised conference is when the delegates have not had to ask for anything – it has already been provided.

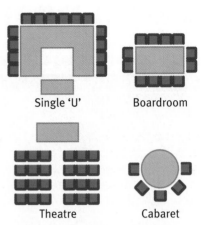

There are several different seating arrangements for conferences

Conferences

Conferences are for business customers. They vary in form and can include:

- large seminars for hundreds of people
- a meeting for as few as three or four people
- promotional events, which can vary from a recruitment or careers fair to the launch of a new product.

Each event will want a different seating plan set up (see the examples shown above), as well as different facilities such as access to the internet, a projector, flipcharts or a large screen for films.

Banquets

Banquets are social events for customers who wish to celebrate an event such as a wedding. Extra facilities are provided for these functions, such as flowers, table decorations and entertainment. These events vary a lot in the format they take. It could be a formal sit-down meal, a buffet or an event where entertainment is more important than food.

Events manager

An events manager will often work independently rather than for a specific venue. Events managers organise weddings but also other celebrations. For weddings, they source and help the customer decide on the:

- venue
- music
- photography or videography
- food
- flowers
- transport
- print design of invites, place names and menus
- designs for table settings, furniture, lighting and staging
- dress
- hair and make-up artists.

ACTIVITY

1 Ed and Mel want to book a wedding meal for 50 people. Write a list of the questions a sales manager needs to ask them to get all the details required to quote a price for the wedding event.

2 A conference manager needs to check a booking for a meeting. The only information provided is the date, the numbers and that they need food. Write a list of questions that need to be asked to make sure the meeting is successful.

CHECK YOUR KNOWLEDGE

1 What does a sales and revenue manager do?

2 What does a conference manager do?

3 What does a banqueting manager do?

4 What does a wedding planner do?

ExamCafé

Exam preparation

Revision checklist

Which exam	Content	What to revise
BOTH	Introduction to employment opportunities	You need to know about the three levels of employment and what their job roles are. You need to understand that some establishments have a formal structure for staff and some an informal structure and know what this means for individual jobs.
CAT	Food and drink service jobs – food preparation	You need to know that different food preparation jobs have different duties and the people carrying out these jobs will have different skills and different training. An understanding of a traditional kitchen structure – a brigade – is also needed.
CAT	Food and drink service – front-of-house	You need to know about the personal and serving skills needed by these staff as well as their knowledge and understanding of food and drink, and you need to know the type of training and qualifications available.
HOS	Accommodation services - front office	You need to know the role the front office plays for a hotel and the different jobs that staff carry out (and the names of these jobs). You need to understand how important verbal and non-verbal communication skills are for people in these jobs, as well as personal appearance.
HOS	Accommodation services – housekeeping	You need to know about the duties of a room attendant and what is included in a cleaning schedule as well as about the job role of a housekeeper.
HOS	Conference and events jobs	You need to know that there are other jobs in the hospitality industry, including those in sales and revenue, conferencing and banqueting and events management. You need to understand the roles and duties for these jobs, especially conferencing.

Common mistakes

You need to understand the difference between skills, duties and role when discussing different hospitality jobs. You also need to understand the type of training on offer for each job.

Activities

Practice writing out what duties a restaurant manager or head chef has to carry out. Practice writing down the skills these people will need to be successful. They are team leaders so their skills will also be relevant to a question about a team leader.

Summarising content

Create a spider diagram of all the different jobs available in the industry. Add the key skills each of these jobs require.

Exam preparation

Sample question

1 There is a range of opportunities in the hospitality and catering industry.

    a Identify one job opportunity in each of the following areas:

        i kitchen, **ii** reception, **iii** restaurant.   (3 marks)

    b Describe the role of the head chef in a large kitchen.   (6 marks)

    c Describe the skills and qualities needed to become a head chef.   (6 marks)

Sample answer

a **i** head chef

  ii receptionist

  iii restaurant manager

Skills are qualifications that show a skill level or past experience that shows a certain skill level. Skills can be operative – such as food preparation, food service or ICT skills. Skills can also be communication skills.

Qualities are a person's personality that help then do the job. These might be listening, motivating and training skills.

b A head chef must be a good chef so that he knows what foods go together and so that he can write good menus. He orders all the food and works out what staff are needed when he does the rotas. A head chef runs the kitchen. He tells people what to do and checks that they are doing it right. He will train staff to make sure they produce food to the correct quality. He will try to encourage his staff to work hard and help them if they have problems. The head chef is responsible for any problems that happen. This includes any hygiene problems so he must make sure staff are trained properly.

c A head chef needs to be highly skilled so he sets a good standard for all the other chefs. He would have a qualification such as City and Guilds or a BTEC. He will have several years experience so will have a wide knowledge of food and a good palate.

A head chef will be very organised so that he orders the right food and has good stock control as well as control over his food budget. He will also be skilled in motivating staff to work hard and be able to work under pressure without shouting at his workers.

Examiner's tip

You need to know the structure of a typical hotel and different job roles to answer this type of question.

A job role is what that person has to do each day or over a few days. If you think about what needs to happen to run a kitchen, you can remember what this job role is.

Examiner's tip

Skills are qualifications that show a skill level or past experience that shows a certain skill level. Skills can be operative – such as food preparation, food service or ICT skills. Skills can also be communication skills.

Qualities are a person's personality that help then do the job. These might be listening, motivating and training skills.

3.1 Food hygiene

Hygiene is all the things we do to maintain cleanliness and prevent disease.

We follow hygiene rules everyday, for example, storing milk, meat and cheese in the fridge, washing hands and cleaning the dishes in hot water.

If we follow hygiene rules, we can make sure that equipment, ourselves and food is free from bacterial **contamination**, which can cause **food poisoning**.

Food hygiene is the good practices that make a clean workplace and workforce for the safe (to eat) production of food.

Unsafe practices lead to contamination – including cross-contamination of food that means that food is unsafe to eat. It will cause illness in people who eat it – food poisoning. Food poisoning can cause death, especially to the high-risk groups.

The high-risk groups more likely to get food poisoning are:
- the very young
- the elderly
- people who are already ill.

Food poisoning trends

There has been an increase in food poisoning over the last few years. This is probably for several reasons, such as:
- more people eating out
- more reheating of ready meals
- more people bulk buying from a supermarket once a week
- a better public awareness about food poisoning (meaning that more is reported).

Hygiene and business

The cost of the food, choice of menu, service, ambience and location are all important reasons why hospitality operations are successful or not. However, hygiene may be the most important reason for success or lack of it, as the chart below suggests.

> **KEY TERMS**
>
> **Contamination:** infection, spoiling or pollution of something.
>
> **Food poisoning:** illness caused by eating food that is naturally poisonous, or contaminated with bacteria or chemicals.

> **ACTIVITY**
>
> Do a survey asking different people how important the hygiene of a restaurant is compared to prices, service, atmosphere, etc.

Bad hygiene can close a business!

Good hygiene means:		Bad hygiene means:	
• happy customers	• keep within the law	• unhappy customers	• unhappy staff
• repeat customers	• happy staff	• no repeat customers	• no job!
• making money – profits	• a good reputation.	• losing money	• a bad reputation
		• not within the law	• possibly, closing the business.

What is food poisoning?

Food poisoning is a reaction you may get when you eat contaminated food. Food is contaminated when there is something in it that shouldn't be there.

Bacteria are the most common cause of food poisoning. Bacteria are micro-organisms – living things that are so small that you can only see them under a powerful microscope.

There are thousands of different types of bacteria that do not harm us. In fact, some are very useful, such as the yeast in bread, the bacteria in natural yoghurt and the 'good' bacteria that naturally exist in our intestines that help with digestion.

Some bacteria are harmful and cause illness. These bacteria are called **pathogenic bacteria**.

Most causes of food poisoning are because food eaten has contained large numbers of pathogenic bacteria. Other causes of food poisoning include:

- viruses – micro-organisms that live on and in people, animals and other organisms and can cause diseases
- moulds – micro-organisms that cause food spoilage over time – a natural process
- poisonous plants – berries and toadstools
- chemicals and metals.

The types of bacteria that cause food poisoning come from six main sources:

- people
- air and dust
- animals and insects (pets and pests)
- rubbish and dirt
- raw food, especially meat, poultry, eggs, shellfish and vegetables
- water.

In fact, EVERYWHERE!

So:

- If good personal hygiene is carried out, **people** will not contaminate food.
- If food is covered and the work area clean, food will not be contaminated by **air or dust**.
- If **pets and pests** are prevented from entering a food area, food will not be contaminated by animals and insects.
- If vegetables are washed and **food waste** is quickly removed and if waste bins are kept tidy, clean and covered, food will not be contaminated by **rubbish and dirt**.
- If **raw foods** are bought from reputable suppliers and stored correctly, food will not be contaminated with bacteria.

There are three types of bacteria:

- good bacteria
- spoilage bacteria – this is bacteria created by decomposing food
- pathogenic bacteria – that cause food poisoning.

KEY WORD

Pathogenic bacteria: bacteria that are pathogens. Pathogens can be either bacteria or waste products of the reproduction of bacteria, such as toxins.

FIND OUT

Research newspaper articles about food poisoning cases. Report on what people did wrong that caused the food poisoning.

CHECK YOUR KNOWLEDGE

1 What is hygiene?
2 Who are the people at the highest risk of getting food poisoning?
3 Why are there more food poisoning cases now?
4 What type of bacteria cause food poisoning?

3.2 Bacteria

Bacterial contamination from pathogenic bacteria is the most common cause of food poisoning. In the industry, it is important to understand how bacteria survive and grow so that systems can be put in place to stop this growth and survival.

How bacteria survive and grow

Bacteria need four things to be able to multiply and grow. These are:

- warmth
- food
- moisture
- time.

If you take away these four things, you can slow down or even stop bacteria from growing.

Warmth

The best temperature for bacteria to multiply at is 37°C – body temperature. Most bacteria multiply between 5°C and 63°C – the temperatures between these two are in the DANGER ZONE.

At temperatures colder than 5°C, bacteria grow very slowly or stop growing.

At temperatures higher than 63°C, bacteria die. Food needs to be cooked to 75°C even in its centre – for at least 15 seconds, to make sure that bacteria has been killed.

Some types of bacteria even survive this temperature because of spores. They need to be cooked above 83°C.

Food

Like all living things, bacteria need nutrients to grow. Some foods, called high-risk foods, are more likely to cause food poisoning than others because bacteria are more likely to grow on them. These high-risk foods need to be recognised and handled with special care to prevent food poisoning. Common high-risk foods are ready-to-eat foods which:

- will not be cooked or re-heated before serving
- easily support bacterial growth in the right conditions of warmth, food, moisture, time.

Moisture

Pathogenic bacteria cannot multiply on dry foods. They need moisture to stay alive. Dried foods such as custard powder and gravy powder do not allow bacteria to grow on them.

As soon as liquid is added, they become ideal for growth. They become high-risk foods.

Time

Bacteria grow by a method called binary fission. It means that they divide and multiply. 1 becomes 2, becomes 4, becomes 8, etc.

In ideal conditions – 37°C, bacteria multiply every 10 to 20 minutes.

This means that in five hours 1 bacterium becomes 65, 536 bacteria.

In one and a half hours a bacteria multiplies to 32. So leaving food out to cool for just this time is important. Any longer is dangerous. High-risk food can be left in the danger zone for only 90 minutes.

High-risk foods

- most cooked meat and cooked poultry
- cooked meat products such as meat pies, stews, gravy and soups made from meat stock
- pâtés and spreads made from meat and fish
- milk and eggs (and foods made from these) that have been lightly cooked or not cooked, e.g. mousses and mayonnaise
- shellfish and seafood – including prawns, mussels, scampi and crab
- cooked rice
- raw meat and poultry.

High-risk foods must be handled with care. They must be:

1 transported at a cool temperature and in a way that the packaging is not damaged
2 stored in a fridge until needed for preparation or serving
3 not used after the 'use by' date
4 kept separately from other foods
5 prepared on clean chopping boards with clean knives and utensils – to prevent cross-contamination
6 covered as much as possible during preparation.

Different bacteria

Different types of pathogenic bacteria cause different symptoms. Some bacteria cause symptoms very quickly because they produce toxins – poisons – on the food before it is even eaten. Other bacteria are unusual in that they do not cause vomiting and diarrhoea.

Make sure that you understand these different sources and symptoms of bacteria so that you can prevent contamination, but also to identify an outbreak of food poisoning.

FIND OUT

Use the internet or books to find out more about one particular type of bacteria. Present the information to the rest of your group using presentation software or pictures.

CHECK YOUR KNOWLEDGE

1 What are pathogenic bacteria?
2 What is the danger zone?
3 What happens to bacteria at 37°C?
4 How often do bacteria multiply?
5 What is a high-risk food?

Bacteria	Source	Typical symptoms	Average onset time
Salmonella	raw poultry, eggs, raw meat, milk, animals – including pets, insects, sewage	stomach ache, diarrhoea, vomiting and a fever	12–36 hours
Clostridium perfringens	animal and human excreta, soil, dust, insects, raw meat	stomach ache and diarrhoea, no vomiting	12–18 hours
Staphylococcus aureus	human body – especially nose, mouth, skin and cuts and boils, also raw milk	stomach ache or cramp, vomiting and a low temperature	1– 6 hours
E.coli	human and animal gut, sewage, water, raw meat	stomach ache, fever, diarrhoea, vomiting, kidney damage or failure	12–24 hours or longer
Listeria	soft cheeses and pâtés	flu-like symptoms (causes miscarriages)	weeks or months
Campylobactor	Meat and poultry, milk and animals	bloody diarrhoea, fever, abdominal pain and nausea	48–60 hours
Clostridium Botulinum	tinned meats – if not properly sealed, leftover stews and casseroles – if not heated correctly	difficulty in breathing, paralysis, blurred vision	18–36 hours
Bacillus cereus	cereals, especially rice – not normally considered a high-risk food	can just be sickness and vomiting or diarrhoea also	1–16 hours

3.3 Physical and chemical contamination

Physical contamination

Pests can cause physical contaminatiion – for example, flies in soup, but also biological contamination. Good pest control methods will prevent this.

Food pests are any animal that lives on our food. They contaminate food by:

- eating the food and spreading bacteria from their saliva as they eat, e.g. flies
- leaving droppings, e.g. mice
- carrying bacteria on their bodies, e.g. salmonella bacteria on pigeons
- urinating on foods, e.g. rats urinate as they eat!

Food handlers should be able to recognise signs of food pests but also how to control them and stop an infestation.

ACTIVITY

Make a check-list for a restaurant that the manager can use in the kitchen and restaurant that would identify any problem places that pests could get into the building.

Type of pest	The way in	Signs of pests	What to do
Rodents	Rats and mice gnaw through wood and get through tiny gaps and holes left in walls or around doors.	Small footprints in dust, droppings, nests, holes in walls and doors, gnawed goods or packaging, grease or smear marks.	Keep the food area in good repair, tidy and clean.
Flying insects	These can get in through windows, doors and airbricks.	Adult flies can be seen easily. They often lay eggs on food so these should be looked for.	Electric fly killers can be used, such as an 'Insecticutor'. Fly sprays can be used in certain areas only.
Crawling insects: ants and cockroaches	These pests are so small that they can get in through cracks, under doors and around pipes. Once in a building, they live under units and in cracks.	Small piles of sand or soil made by ants. The insects themselves, eggs, egg cases and moulted 'skins' of cockroaches, as well as droppings.	Insecticides can control these insects.
Birds and domestic animals	Birds are attracted by food left out for them. Cats and dogs are attracted too.	These are very large! Other signs of their presence are similar to rodents – droppings, holes in walls, gnawed goods etc.	Pets should not be allowed in food rooms. Birds should not be encouraged by leaving food out for them as they carry salmonella and campylobacter.

Objects

'Objects' can get into food, making it unsafe to eat at any time from field to plate.

Stage	Objects	How to prevent contamination
Picking	Stones, twigs, slugs and caterpillars.	Wash fruit and especially vegetables.
Manufacture	Nuts, bolts and other pieces of equipment and also glass.	Ensure a clean, clear work area.
Food preparation	Stones, pips, leaves, stalks, bones and parts of shell (nut or fish) and fish scales. Parts of packaging, such as string, elastic bands and cardboard, dust and dirt.	Packaging is thrown away quickly.
Food handling	Jewellery, hair, fingernails, cutlery, money, buttons and pen tops.	Maintain good, personal hygiene practices.

Chemical contamination

The main chemical contamination that can occur is by cleaning chemicals. It is important to follow the manufacturer's instructions on how to use and store these. There must be a separate cupboard for cleaning materials – away from food. The cleaning chemicals must be stored in secure, clearly labelled containers – preferably the original container they were bought in. *If you use too little of the chemical – it won't be effective at the job. If you use too much – it doesn't mean that it will be more effective, it could be difficult to rinse off and then contaminate food.*

Other chemical contamination can come from:

- pesticides sprayed onto fruit and vegetables – wash them
- pest control bait – bait must be either covered or under worktops so that it does not come into contact with food or workers
- some plastic containers (release chemicals into food)
- some cooking pans (release metals into food).

Food must be 'fit to eat' – (food means food and drink – even a cup of tea).

Food is unsafe if it is:

- unfit for human consumption – if it contains, for example, a fly
- so contaminated that it would be unreasonable to expect it to be eaten or drunk in that state
- made harmful to health by adding or removing something from it, or by using unsuitable handling techniques
- not of the nature, substance or quality demanded by the customer – if, for example, a steak pie is a chicken pie
- falsely or misleadingly described or presented – if dried packet soup is sold as home-made.

Food safety laws require that hospitality businesses make sure that staff:

- practice high standards of personal hygiene
- have regular training in hygiene and safety
- obey the requirements of the food legislation that relates to them.

This legislation recommends that hospitality organisations have a food safety policy that will include:

- standards of personal food hygiene
- procedures for reporting illness and accidents
- pest control requirements
- minimum acceptable standards of cleaning and disinfecting food areas
- requirements for visitors into food production areas.

ACTIVITY

Produce an A5 mini-poster that gives clear guidelines about how to use cleaning chemicals. Start it off with: Stop! Have you ...?

CHECK YOUR KNOWLEDGE

1 Give five examples of physical contamination.

2 Give two examples of chemical contamination.

3 Explain the two ways to prevent pests contaminating food.

4 What does food safety mean?

3.4 Personal hygiene

Personal hygiene is key to good hygiene practices. The main cause of food poisoning outbreaks is poor hand washing.

Hand washing

Some 'when's are common sense, others you might not have thought about. The list is long:

- after you have been to the toilet
- when you enter a food area – after a break or at the beginning of your work or lesson
- if you have touched your face – especially your nose, ears or mouth (nearly half of us have the Staphylococcus Aureus bacteria)
- after handling rubbish (includes food rubbish but also outside packaging)
- after cleaning and disinfecting the work area (if you use antibacterial cleaner at the start of your work)
- after you have handled raw foods
- after you have touched a pet.

Bacteria isn't just on fingertips, it is all over the hands so all of the hand needs to be cleaned.

1. Always use *warm* water. Wet before applying soap.
2. Apply soap.
3. Rub hands together vigorously counting to 15.

Rub:

- both sides
- around thumbs
- between each finger
- under nails.

4. Rinse with clean water.
5. Dry thoroughly with a clean dry towel, paper towel or air dryer.
6. Turn off the tap with a paper towel – if possible.

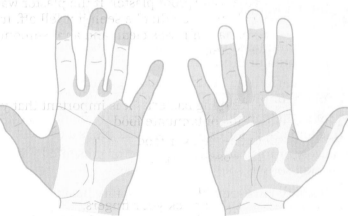

- ▨ Areas most frequently missed during hand washing
- ☐ Less frequently missed
- ▨ Not missed

Clothing

Clothes, including shoes, can bring dirt and bacteria into a food area. Wearing clean clothes prevents this.

The best thing is to leave outdoor cloths away from food areas. Wear clean clothes when working with food. These clothes are often called protective clothing – you wear it to protect the food from you!

Clothes should be:

- light coloured – to show the dirt
- long-sleeved – to prevent the skin from touching food
- no pockets – so nothing can fall into food
- non-removable fasteners such as VelcroTM and press studs – NOT BUTTONS.

Disposable aprons should be worn when working with raw meat/poultry and eggs so that they can be easily removed and thrown away.

Hats or hairnets should be worn if you are cooking for others as on average you lose 100 hairs a day. Otherwise, hair should be clean and tied up.

Other points

- It is easier to keep your hands clean if you have short nails. Nailbrushes can clean under nails but it is better to keep nails short. Nail varnish should not be worn, as this can chip off and also hide dirty nails.
- Rings and watches should not be worn, as dirt can collect in these and bacteria can live on or under them.
- In industry, some people are permitted to keep their wedding ring on if they cover it with a blue plaster.
- Make up, perfume or aftershave can taint food and make it smell.

Skin and plasters

Even clean skin has bacteria living on it. Bacteria in the pores of your skin cause spots. So, all cuts, grazes and sores must be covered with a blue waterproof plaster. If the plaster was the usual skin pink colour, it couldn't be seen if it fell off. It would look like a piece of ham if it was clean and a mushroom if it was dirty. Blue is better.

Habits

As you might be carrying bacteria, it is important that you don't do anything to contaminate food.

1 Don't cough or sneeze over food.
2 Don't pick your nose.
3 Don't smoke.
4 Don't eat or chew gum.
5 Don't bite your nails or lick your fingers.
6 Don't taste with your finger – taste food with a clean spoon.

Fitness for work

Fitness for work means that you must not be suffering from, or carrying an illness or disease that could cause a problem with food safety, if you are involved in food preparation for others.

If you have a cold, a sore throat or an ear infection, you are more likely to pass harmful bacteria onto food.

If you have diarrhoea or vomiting you could have food poisoning. Even if sickness and diarrhoea has stopped, you can still carry harmful bacteria in your gut for 48 hours afterwards.

ACTIVITY

List all the bad habits that you have seen food workers exhibit. Discuss these habits in a group so that you find out which bad habits are most common. Design a training poster for these bad habits that explain why they should be dropped.

CHECK YOUR KNOWLEDGE

1 When should you wash your hands?
2 How should you wash your hands?
3 Why is it important to not sneeze over food?
4 Why should you wear a hairnet if you are cooking for others?
5 What does fitness for work mean?

3.5 Food storage, preparation, cooking and cleaning

Good personal hygiene is a major part of good food hygiene but carrying out correct storage, preparation and cooking of food is also very important.

Storage

There are four key points about storage:

1. Rotate stock so that old supplies of food are used before new stock is used. The system of 'First in first out' (FIFO) should be used.
2. Use food before the use by date. These foods have a short shelf life and are more likely to contain bacteria or spoil quickly. Foods eaten after the use by date could be unsafe to eat. It is illegal to sell food after its 'use by'. Foods with 'best before' dates can be eaten after this date but probably won't taste as good as they should do.
3. Chilled foods must be kept below 8°C. High-risk foods must be 5°C or below. Food should be chilled to below 5°C within 90 minutes. If hot food is put into a fridge straight away, the temperature rises. This causes condensation that could contaminate other foods.
4. Raw and ready-to-eat foods should be stored separately. Ideally, there should be separate fridges for these two types of foods as this will help to prevent bacteria spreading between these foods.

Preparation

Good preparation is all about preventing cross-contamination. Cross-contamination is when bacteria are transferred from a contaminated source to a ready-to-eat food. Cross-contamination can be:

- direct – for example, raw food touching cooked or blood dripping
- indirect – for example, from a knife, a chopping board or a hand.

'Vehicles' help bacteria travel.

Usual vehicles are: hands, utensils and equipment and handles of doors, fridges and cupboards or taps.

Using colour-coded chopping boards for preparation will help with this prevention:

- BLUE for raw fish
- RED for raw meat and poultry
- YELLOW for cooked meat
- GREEN for fruit and salad ingredients
- WHITE for dairy and bread
- BROWN for vegetables.

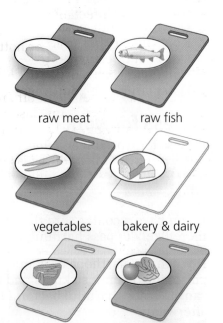

raw meat   raw fish

vegetables   bakery & dairy

cooked meat   Salad and fruit

Cooking

Some foods need to be treated with extra care while they are cooked to make sure that they are safe to eat. These include eggs, shellfish, rice and pulses such as red kidney beans.

Some foods must be thoroughly cooked to make sure any harmful bacteria are killed.

Raw meat and poultry are often the main source of bacteria in a kitchen. So meat needs sealing when cooked – to kill any surface bacteria and needs turning during cooking – to cook evenly. It must then be checked in different ways with a temperature probe or skewer to make sure that it is cooked all the way through.

Cross-contamination can happen when grilling or barbecuing. If raw meat is added to a grill where food is already cooking and this raw meat touches or drips onto the cooking food, bacteria can spread and stop it being safe to eat.

Cleaning

Cleaning is the process of making something free of dirt and contamination. It involves the use of energy – your own or a machine's, such as a dishwasher.

Detergents are used to help dissolve grease and remove dirt. The use of a detergent, energy and hot water will kill some pathogenic bacteria but most will survive. To prevent bacteria causing food poisoning, items and equipment must be disinfected after cleaning.

Disinfection is the reduction of bacteria to a low, safe level. It can be achieved by the use of:
- chemical disinfectants
- steam
- very hot water at 82°C or hotter.

Heat and chemical disinfection are often combined.

Disinfectants do not clean off grease and dirt so must be used after cleaning. They must also be left on the surface long enough to work properly – 'contact time'.

Sanitisers combine a detergent and a disinfectant. They clean and disinfect if there is enough 'contact time'.

'Clear and clean as you go' system

Always keeping your kitchen clear and clean is the best way to make it safe. A 'clean and clear as you go' system does this and is exactly what it says.

A cleaning schedule is a useful way to control effective cleaning in a food area. The schedule should include what needs cleaning, how it should be cleaned and how often.

CHECK YOUR KNOWLEDGE

1 What does FIFO mean?
2 Can you eat food after its use by date?
3 Give two examples of direct and indirect cross-contamination.
4 What is a green chopping board used for?
5 What four types of food need to be cooked carefully?
6 How would you make sure that meat is cooked safely?
7 What is a sanitiser?

3.6 Food safety and health and safety legislation

Customers need a safe environment to enjoy their hospitality experience. Workers need to work in a safe environment to enable them to continue to work and work in the best way possible.

Food safety legislation

Food safety means the protection of consumer health and well-being by safeguarding food from anything that can cause harm.

There is a wide variety of UK and EU legislation relevant to the hospitality industry. For example, there are specific regulations about eggs, ice cream and meat preparation. The most important law is the Food Safety Act 1990.

CASE STUDY

16 Year Old Employee Flash Fries Arm in 360°F Oil Following Slip

A 16 year old girl was employed at a fast food outlet to cook fries at a frying range. Severe burns from simple slipping accident

She slipped on water leaking from an ice-making machine and instinctively put out her hand to break her fall. Unfortunately her hand went into the deep fat fryer containing oil at a temperature of 360°F and she sustained severe burns to her left hand and forearm.

The outlet was short staffed on the day of the accident and the Team Leader was working on the tills instead of monitoring workplace safety.

Although the company policy was to mop up spillages it was common practice to leave spillages at busy times and cover them with a sheet of cardboard, which itself can create a tripping hazard. At busy times it was usual to give greater priority to serving customers than to cleaning spillages.

The ice-making machine had been leaking for several days and various attempts had been made by different contractors to cure the leak. No-one had sole responsibility to co-ordinate the repair of faulty equipment and a lack of communication between different shift managers left the equipment leaking over a long period of time.

Following the accident, the company did a complete review of its management of wet/contaminated floors.

- Slip control was given priority over serving customers
- Systems were put in place to ensure maintenance of faulty equipment
- Managers were identified as having responsibility to ensure slips procedures were implemented and followed
- Employees empowered to deal with slips as a priority and given backing by company
- Extra training on slips procedures was given to all staff

The local authority prosecuted the company and on successful conviction the magistrates imposed a total fine of £15000. The investigating Environmental Health Officer believed that the accident was completely avoidable as the company had failed to maintain a safe system of work or to carry out a suitable and sufficient assessment of the risks associated with slipping within the kitchen.

This places the responsibility for safe food on staff working at each stage of production – from farm to table.

Remember that food can be made harmful – be contaminated biologically – by harmful bacteria and moulds but also physically and chemically.

Health and safety legislation

The **Health and Safety at Work Act 1974** tries to make sure that charges as stated in the case study opposite are brought when needed.

Employers or management have the main responsibility in setting a health and safety policy and making sure that all the legislation in the act is carried out. Management must:

- make sure that the workplace is regularly monitored for health and safety
- provide equipment that is not a risk to health
- provide safe storage for substances that could be a risk to safety
- provide a written safety policy and make sure that workers know about it and see it
- make sure that work practices are safe
- provide enough information and training for staff.

Workers must:

- take reasonable care for their own health and safety
- make sure that other people are not put in danger because of their actions – including what they don't do
- comply with the safety rules and practices that go with the job they are doing, for example, not interfere with or misuse anything provided to protect their safety
- report all fire and safety hazards to their immediate boss
- co-operate with the company so regulations can be followed
- wear as instructed any protective clothing
- report all injuries or dangerous incidents
- attend training sessions and safety meetings if required.

The Health and Safety at Work Act is an 'umbrella' act, which means that it also includes other important regulations which relate to health and safety. Regulations such as:

- COSHH – Control of Substances Hazardous to Health – such as cleaning chemicals
- Fire safety 2005
- Manual handling operations regulations 1992

Establishments make sure that they comply with this act by carrying out a **risk assessment**. See Chapter 3.9 for more on this.

KEY TERM

Risk assessment: This is a calculation of the risk level for a task or in an area such as the workplace

FIND OUT

Use the internet or books to find out more about the acts in this topic and what they mean to workers.

CHECK YOUR KNOWLEDGE

1 What did the owner of the hotel in Skegness do wrong?
2 Why do you think there is a Health and Safety at Work Act?
3 Why is the Health and Safety at Work Act an umbrella act?

3.7 Working safely 1

The Health and Safety at Work Act tries to make sure that accidents don't happen.

The legislation requires employers to carry out a risk assessment (see Chapter 3.9) and to provide safety signs on any workplace risk that is not satisfactorily controlled by other means.

Safety signs

The term 'safety sign' includes various types of warning sign. The signs are telling you to do or not do different things. Some safety signs are temporary, for example, a wet floor sign. Others are permanent.

STOP

These are prohibition or danger signs. They tell you something you 'MUST NOT DO'.

They are:
- round shape
- black pictogram, white background, red edging and red diagonal line.

Examples: No Smoking, No Entry, No Naked Lights.

DANGER

These are warning signs. They warn you of a hazard or danger. They are:
- triangular shape
- black pictogram on a yellow background with black edging.

Examples: Deep Water, Forklift Trucks operating, Electricity, Toxic Substances.

OBEY

These are mandatory signs. They tell you something you 'MUST DO'. They are:
- round shape
- white pictogram on a blue background.

Examples: Wear Protective Clothing, Hard Hat Area, Keep Fire Doors Shut, Wash Your Hands, Fire Action.

FIRE

These are for fire equipment. They are used to mark and indicate the location of fire equipment. They are:
- rectangular or square shape
- white pictogram on a red background

Examples: Fire Extinguisher, Fire Point, Fire Hose.

SAFETY

These are used to mark the presence of safe exit routes or locations of safety equipment. They are:
- rectangular or square shape
- white pictogram on a green background

Examples: First Aid, Emergency/Fire Exit.

Fire safety

Fire is very dangerous and can easily become life threatening. You need to know what to do in the event of fire. You also need to understand how a fire is started, especially as fires can easily start in kitchens.

Preventing fire

Fire needs three things to burn. As soon as one thing is removed, the fire goes out.

Fuel: fire has to be fed and uses any substance that burns, such as gas, electricity, cloth, oil or wood. Once this fuel has been used up, the fire goes out.

Air: fire requires oxygen (part of air) to keep going. If air is removed, the fire goes out. This is why a fire blanket can put a fire out.

Heat: fire creates heat. If the heat of the fire is removed, the fire goes out. This is how many fire extinguishers work.

So, a fire can be put out by:
1 starving it of fuel
2 smothering it by removing air
3 cooling it by taking away heat.

Fire triangle

Fires do not necessarily need to be 'ignited'. There is an 'auto ignition temperature' – the temperature at which combustion takes place without the introduction of an ignition source. Typical examples include: chip pans, compost heaps, oily rags or scraps from the fish and chip shop.

Dealing with a fire

You need to know the steps to take if a fire does start:
- Do not panic – try to remain calm.
- Sound the fire alarm.
- Contact the fire brigade. Do not wait for the fire to get out of control before calling the emergency services.
- Warn other people that there is a fire.
- If possible, turn off gas and electrical supplies.
- Close (not lock) all doors/windows – this will help to slow the fire down.
- If the fire is small and localised and can be extinguished quickly and safely, without risk to yourself or others, use the appropriate fire-fighting equipment.
- Evacuate in an orderly fashion, using the nearest safest exit to the assembly point.
- Do not use lifts.

ACTIVITY

Visit a local hotel or guesthouse (or watch a video showing establishments). List (or photograph) all the safety signs and fire extinguishers you find on a rough plan of the establishment. Analyse how safe you think the establishment is.

Fire extinguishers

Make sure that you know about the different types of fire extinguishers and when they should be used:

Type	Works by	Best for	Not for
Water extinguisher	Cooling burning material	Fire involving solids – woods, cloth, plastics, coal, etc	Electrical appliances, burning fat or oil
CO_2 extinguisher	Replacing oxygen in the air and smothering the flame	Liquids such as fat and oil, electrical appliances	Confined spaces. Does not cool fire well. Check it does not restart
Foam extinguisher	Smothering fire with a blanket of foam	A few liquid fires	Not for use in the home, or on fat or oil
Fire blanket	Smothering burning material by cutting out air	Fat pan fires on the cooker, wrapping round someone whose clothes are on fire, kitchen fires	General use

CHECK YOUR KNOWLEDGE

1 What shape and colour is an obey sign?

2 What colour and sign is a danger sign?

3 What three things are needed for a fire?

4 Why would you use a fire blanket for a chip pan fire?

3.8 Working safely 2

Many accidents are caused by poor work methods. The most common hazards that cause accidents are:

- sharp objects such as knives and slicing machine blades
- slippery floors
- tripping over items
- hot liquids such as frying oil, and boiling water
- moving heavy items, such as sacks of potatoes or drums of oil.

These risks can be controlled by:
- using a non-slip floor and cleaning up spillages straight away
- training staff to use equipment correctly
- having rules about leaving out large items on the floor
- maintaining equipment
- providing protective clothing
- providing trolleys to move heavy items safely
- training staff on how to lift heavy items.

Lifting heavy objects

The correct way to lift and carry objects is:
- Shoulders should be back.
- Back is straight. Bend knees to get hold of object.
- Chin is tucked in.
- Get a firm grip of the object.
- Hands should be level with waist.
- The object should be held close to the body.

First Aid

There are designated first aiders in every workplace. These are people who have had training in first aid procedures. They are the first people who will help if there has been an accident but everybody can know about basic first aid procedures.

How to deal with bleeding, burns and shock

If there is **bleeding**:
- Wash and dry your own hands.
- Clean the cut by running under water.
- Pat dry with a sterile dressing.
- Cover the cut with a sterile dressing.

CASE STUDY

Peter, a new chef in a hotel in Birmingham had just finished making a beef stock in a pan that was 1 metre wide. He tried to lift the pan off the hob by himself, but only managed to lift it for a few seconds before he got a sharp shooting pain in his back. He is off work for a month. He did not follow instructions given to him on his induction day at the hotel.

- What should Peter have done to avoid his injury?

ACTIVITY

Design a poster to be used in a hotel kitchen that explains how to correctly lift heavy boxes.

If there is severe bleeding, carry out the above, then:

• Apply direct pressure to the wound with a pad.
• Raise and support the injured limb.
• Treat the casualty for shock.
• Bandage the wound but not too tightly.
• Dial 999.

A **burn** is an injury to tissue caused by heat, electricity, chemicals or friction. A **scald** is a type of burn caused by hot liquid or steam.

To treat a minor burn, hold the affected area under running cold water for at least 10 minutes. If a minor burn is larger than a postage stamp, it will need medical attention.

Larger burns still need this medical attention but the person will also need treatment for shock. Cover the burn with a clean, non-fluffy material, such as a plastic bag or cling film to protect from infection.

This is the position for **shock**. If a person is pale, cold, has shallow breathing, a rapid pulse or is yawning, put them into this position.

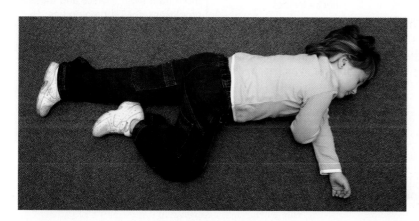

This is the **recovery position**. If a person is unconscious, put them into this position. It is important that their airway is open. This can be done by lifting the chin forward and adjusting the hand under the chin.

FIND OUT

What does a first aider learn during their training.

CHECK YOUR KNOWLEDGE

1 What are the most common causes of accidents?
2 What is the correct way to lift a heavy object?
3 What is a scald?
4 What are the symptoms of shock?

3.9 Risk assessment and HACCP

Hospitality establishments make sure that they comply with the Health and Safety Act by carrying out a risk assessment.

The five steps of risk assessment

In a business, there are five steps to risk assessment:

STEP 1: Identify the hazard. For example: liquids that could spill easily, rapid movement of people around the kitchen, stacking of delivery items, use of electrical equipment.

STEP 2: Decide who might be harmed and how. For example: members of staff, customers or delivery staff. They might collide, have hot oil spilt on them, fall over boxes or get an electric shock.

STEP 3: Evaluate the risks, such as how likely is it to happen, and decide on the precautions. For example: how often are there deliveries, how often is the electrical equipment serviced, how often is hot oil spilt on the floor? Also, is there a maximum safe height for boxes to be stacked, is there a procedure for cleaning up spillages and is there a proper workflow system in use in a kitchen?

STEP 4: Record the findings and implement them. For example: arrange regular maintenance of equipment, put warning signs up, train staff in the correct use of equipment and the correct workflow in the kitchen.

STEP 5: Review the assessment and update if necessary. For example: have regular health and safety meetings that include six monthly reviews of all risk assessments.

Is its use necessary?	Who is at risk?	How are they at risk?	What precautions need to be taken?	Does it need to be recorded?	What review will take place?
Yes, to produce large quantities of food.	Chef – pastry and commis cleaner.	Tripping over large equipment. Broken limbs, because of no guard. Electric shock and fire because of faulty wiring.	Position mixer securely and out of the way. Check electrics. Ensure regular maintenance. Position warning signs and details of proper use. Make sure that guards are fitted. Only trained staff use the equipment.	Yes – by law – if there are more than five employees.	Check all controls are in place and that training has taken place. Have regular maintenance.

A risk assessment example: Use of a food mixer in a restaurant kitchen

Risk assessments should be updated regularly. An effective risk assessment system helps a business because it:

- helps to prevent accidents
- makes it easier to carry out work
- can improve the standard of work produced
- fulfils legal requirements.

HACCP

HACCP means Hazard Analysis Critical Control Points. This process helps you look at how you handle food and introduce procedures to make sure that the food you produce is safe to eat. Every business that produces, serves or sells food is required to have a documented system highlighting all areas where special attention should be paid to food safety.

The HACCP system should cover the route from delivery of raw materials through to the consumption, service or sale of food.

The easiest way to explain this is in the following chart.

TRY THIS

Write a risk assessment and a HACCP plan for an event you are about to run.

Step	Hazard	Action
1 Purchase	High-risk food contaminated with pathogenic bacteria	Buy from reputable supplier.
2 Receipt of food	High-risk food contaminated with pathogenic bacteria	Check the temperature is right – below 5°C for high-risk foods. Check it looks, smells and feels right.
3 Storage	Growth of pathogenic bacteria on high-risk foods further contamination	High-risk foods stored at below 5°C. Stock rotation. Use food before use by date.
4 Preparation	Contamination of high-risk foods Growth of pathogenic bacteria	Maintain good personal hygiene standards. Maintain good cleaning schedules. Separate cooked and raw foods. Leave high-risk foods in danger zone for less than 90 minutes.
5 Cooking	Survival of pathogenic bacteria	Cook food so that the middle is above 75°C for more than 15 seconds. Sear (brown) meat at the start of cooking.
6 Cooling	Growth of pathogenic bacteria contamination with pathogenic bacteria	Cool food as quickly as possible – to below 5°C within 90 minutes. Cover food.
7 Hot-holding	Growth of pathogenic bacteria	Keep food hot – above 63°C.
8 Reheating	Survival of pathogenic bacteria	Reheat to above 75°C.
9 Chilled storage	Growth of pathogenic bacteria	Keep high-risk foods at below 5°C. Rotate stock.
10 Serving	Growth of pathogenic bacteria contamination	Maintain good personal hygiene standards. Serve cold and hot high-risk foods as quickly as possible so that they do not get warm or cool down.

HACCP has seven steps:

1 Identify what could go wrong (the hazards).
2 Identify the most important points where things can go wrong (the critical control points – CCPs).
3 Set critical limits at each CCP (e.g. cooking temperature/time).
4 Set up checks at CCPs to prevent problems occurring (monitoring).
5 Decide what to do if something goes wrong (corrective action).
6 Prove that the HACCP Plan is working (verification).
7 Keep records of all of the above (documentation).

A HACCP plan must be kept up to date. It needs to be reviewed from time to time, especially whenever something in the food operation changes.

CHECK YOUR KNOWLEDGE

1 Give two examples of possible hazards you would include in a risk assessment and how you would prevent them from happening.

2 Why does writing a risk assessment help a business?

3 Why should you buy food from a reputable supplier? What do you think reputable supplier means?

ExamCafé

Exam preparation

Revision checklist

Which exam	Content	What to revise
All for Catering but some background information is required for Hospitality	Food hygiene	You need to understand why good food hygiene practices are important and what happens if an establishment has bad hygiene practices. You need to know what food poisoning is and how it can happen.
	Bacteria	You need to understand what bacteria need to grow and survive and that there are different bacteria that are found on different foods and other sources. That these bacteria cause different symptoms.
	Food safety	You need to know that there is physical and chemical contamination as well as biological and that pests cause physical and biological contamination. You need to know about food safety legislation and who is responsible for what.
	Personal hygiene	You need to know how important hand washing is as well as all the other important personal hygiene points including bad habits and fitness for work.
	Food storage, preparation, cooking and cleaning	You need to know the correct methods of storing, preparing and cooking food as well as how to clean correctly.
	Health and safety legislation	You need to know about the health and safety act, what managers are responsible for and what workers are responsible for.
	Working safely	You need to know about the different safety signs and when to use them. You need to know how to prevent a fire and how to deal with different fires. You also need to know about how to lift heavy objects correctly and about first aid procedures for cuts and burns.
	Risk Assessment and HACCP	You need to know about the five steps of risk assessment and what HACCP is.

Activities

This is a knowledge-based unit of work that needs learning. Temperatures, times and different types of bacteria, as well as all safety information, all need remembering.

Exam preparation

Use past exam questions to check your knowledge. Most of these questions are about your knowledge and do not ask you to apply this knowledge to a particular situation.

Sample question

1 Maintaining a safe environment for customers and staff is everyone's responsibility.
   a Identify three of the employers responsibilities under the Health and Safety at Work Act. (3 marks)
   b Muscle and back injuries can happen easily.
      Give detailed instructions to be included in a leaflet for a new member of staff regarding the correct procedure for lifting a heavy box. (3 marks)

Sample answer

a
- Provide enough information and training for staff
- Provide equipment which is not a risk to health
- Provide safe storage for substances that could be a risk to safety

b
- The correct way to lift and carry objects is:
- Shoulders should be back.
- Back is straight.
- Bend knees to get hold of object.
- Chin is tucked in.
- A firm grip of the object.
- Hands level with waist.
- The object should be held close to the body.

2 The Royal hotel is catering for a wedding of 150 guests. As food safety is essential, special care has to be taken regarding cleanliness, temperature and contamination in order to prevent food poisoning. Discuss how the hotel staff can ensure the food is safe to eat during:

a	Preparation of food	(6 marks)
b	Storing food prior to serving	(6 marks)
c	Serving the food	(6 marks)

Sample answer

a The chefs should make sure that they are clean, wash their hands and wear their uniform. Their nails should be short. And they need to have their basic food hygiene certificate. They must not cough over the food. The chopping boards must be clean and knives cleaned every time they are used.

b High-risk food must not be left out at room temperature for longer than 90 minutes. Food must be cooled rapidly using a chiller. It must be stored in a fridge at less than 5°C. Once food has been prepared it must be covered and labelled, also raw and cooked food kept separate.

c The staff should be clean and hygienic in the way they work. They should not touch their face or hair and not cough or they could contaminate the food with Staphylococcus Aureus bacteria. They need to make sure the food has been cooked to 75°C for 15 seconds and then hot held above 63°C. Cold food should be served quickly and serving equipment cleaned. Staff should know what is in each dish so they can check with customers if they have any allergies.

Chapter 4

SPECIALIST EQUIPMENT

4.1 Small equipment

Small equipment can either be hand-held items or small pieces of equipment that can be sited on top of a work surface. Examples of these can include chefs' knives, colour-coded chopping boards, and a whole range of small equipment, including peelers and pastry cutters, through to small electrical appliances.

Knives

There are two main types of knives, carbon steel and stainless steel. The carbon steel knife gets a better edge when sharpened. However, it is prone to rust. The stainless steel knives are more popular but it is more difficult to get a good edge.

When sharpening knives, either a steel, a knife grinder or a whetstone can be used to get a good edge.

There is a huge variety of knives with varying styles, makes and sizes. Here are some of the more common types:

- **Boning knife:** used by butchers to remove bones from selected cuts of meat and poultry. It has a firm narrow blade and is used to go in between the bones.
- **Filleting knife:** used to fillet fish and has a flexible narrow blade.
- **Cook's knife:** a general purpose knife and can be used to great effect to chop vegetables into a variety of cuts.
- **Utility knife:** a small preparation knife.
- **Carving knife:** can either be serrated or smooth and is used in a smooth sawing action to carve roast cuts of meat.

A range of knives used by cooks

Knife safety

Knives should be securely stored to prevent injury. Storage can include use of knife-blocks or magnetic wall racks. If knives are transported they must be carried in an appropriate case or knife wallet.

Chopping boards

As a general rule, chopping boards can either be wooden or plastic. Many catering establishments opt for the plastic ones as these give them the option to go for colour-coded chopping boards. See Chapter 3.5 for a list of colour-coded chopping boards.

Blenders and food processors

Hand blenders

Domestic hand blenders can be used to blend soups and sauces in addition to batters. However, when blending large catering quantities, a specialist industrial hand blender is required.

Liquidisers

The same rule applies for liquidisers as for hand blenders. When the number of customers increases, the size and the sturdiness of the equipment must increase also. Liquidisers can be used for soups and sauces.

Food processors

Food processors have a multitude of possible applications, including liquidising, chopping, mincing, slicing and grating. They have a variety of attachments suited for each task. This item of equipment should be used when bulk preparations are required. For example, chopping a small amount of vegetables requires the same setting up, use and cleaning down of the machine as for a large amount. It would take a few minutes to chop the small number of vegetables in the conventional way.

Mixing machines

Mixing machines generally use either a whisk attachment or a dough hook. Products like meringue, bread dough and pastry can be made for large numbers of people depending on the size of machine. Other attachments include a mincer or blender, again depending on the type.

General small equipment

To assist the caterer, there is a whole range of small equipment available including:

- **Pallet knife:** this is a small flat knife with no edges used to pick up items.
- **Peeler:** this can either be a general peeler or speed peeler.
- **Mandolin:** a professional slicing implement with adjustable blades used to cut up vegetables.
- **Pastry cutters:** a huge variety of styles and shapes is available for the caterer.
- **Specialist cutters:** for example a parisienne cutter also known as a melon baller.
- **Spatulas:** plastic utensils used to scrape the last ingredients from a bowl or tray.

A pallet knife and peeler

4.2 Large equipment

Large equipment is generally fixed items of machinery that can be gas, electric or a combination of both.

Ovens

Industrial ovens can be purchased as light, medium or heavy duty. Either way, these ovens are far sturdier than their domestic counterparts. The ovens are designed to accommodate huge roasting trays and cater for large numbers of customers. The oven can either be gas or electric and some can include an **induction hob**. This uses electromagnetic induction to heat a pan and requires special pans, but the advantage to the caterer is the instant heat transfer that induction provides.

The main oven can either be a standard oven range or accommodate a **convection** oven unit. The advantage of a convection oven (fan assisted) is the even transfer of heat around the products and a quicker cooking time.

It is important to note that there are different types of ovens, including pizza and tandoor ovens used to support different cultural cuisines.

KEY TERMS

Induction hob: uses a magnetic field with an induction coil to produce heat.

Convection oven: uses forced air (usually via a fan) to distribute heat evenly around the oven.

All kitchens feature equipment for frying

Fryers

These are industrial standard frying units with either single or double tanks that can be secured to the floor for safety. They are thermostatically controlled and most feature a timer unit.

Bain-maries

A bain-marie is a pan or bath of hot water. For example, in its basic sense, a bowl placed over a pan of hot water for melting chocolate is a bain marie. In a commercial environment, it could either be a cupboard used to keep

FIND OUT

Go to your school or college and find out how catering staff use a bain-marie for the lunchtime service.

food items warm, or a large water bath used to place large containers of food items to keep warm.

Fridges

In a large establishment, it is highly likely that a walk-in refrigerator would be used to store food items. This would feature separate sections/shelves to isolate meat, vegetables and other food products. A walk-in fridge should have an external and internal temperature gauge, in addition to an internal handle release to prevent employees being trapped inside! In some establishments, an additional dairy and fish fridge might be an option as fish can taint other foods and dairy is very susceptible to strong smelling foods.

Freezers

In a similar way to the walk-in refrigerators, there are also walk-in freezers, which can be used to separate different frozen food stuffs.

Dishwashers

A domestic dishwasher simply would not handle the sheer volume of dirty crockery, cutlery and other items in a commercial setting. In a hotel, for example, dishes are loaded into racks, which are slid into the dishwasher and up to 50 racks per hour is not uncommon. Compare this to the cycle of a normal domestic dishwasher where one load can take over an hour. Some commercial dishwashers have a conveyor-belt system where racks are loaded with dirty crockery at one end, which is clean on reaching the other end.

Commercial dishwashers need to be efficient enough to clean the items put through the machine, hot enough to kill bacteria and fast enough to cope with the demands of the restaurant.

Grills, griddles and salamanders

Sometimes confusion occurs in a catering kitchen when a **salamander** is referred to as a grill.

The grill can be charcoal with the heat coming from below. Items such as steak, fish and vegetables can all be grilled, leaving an attractive mark and smoky flavour.

A griddle unit leaves a similar mark to the grill without the open flames.

ACTIVITY

On an A4 piece of paper, do a rough design of a kitchen suitable for serving 60 people in a public house. Put items of equipment needed on the sheet and label them. Give reasons for your choice on the other side of the paper.

KEY TERM

Salamander: a grill in which the heat comes from above (as in a domestic oven grill).

CHECK YOUR KNOWLEDGE

1 What are the advantages of an industrial oven?

2 What is a bain-marie?

3 Why should a large establishment have a walk-in fridge?

4.3 Food service equipment

The equipment required for food service needs to be appropriate to clientele, for example, a food display unit would not look out of place in a cafeteria and a guéridon trolley would not look out of place in a gourmet restaurant. This section covers not only the equipment used to assist food service but also small pieces of equipment, such as crockery and cutlery.

Large equipment

Guéridon trolley

A guéridon trolley, also known as a flambé trolley is a portable waiter/waitress station used for the cooking or finishing of flambé items. For example, in the preparation of crêpe Suzette the pancakes would already be made but the person making the pancakes would make the suzette sauce, heat the pancakes in the sauce and serve directly to the customers at the table.

Coffee machines

Filter coffee can be made either using a cafetiere or commercial coffee filter machine. This is where a filter and the coffee is placed into a filter pan and water is drip-fed into a decanter. The fresh coffee is kept warm for a limited period of time via a built-in heater.

Espresso and cappuccino machines

A large number of machines are available, some at great cost to the caterer, to make a variety of speciality drinks, including latte, espresso and cappuccino.

TRY THIS

Find a recipe for either crêpe Suzette or Steak Diane. Practice making your choice in front of your fellow students, taking care to prepare, cook and serve as though you are working in a restaurant.

Espresso and cappuccino machines are becoming increasingly popular in offices and workplaces

58

Food display unit

In a large canteen, you may find a specialist unit with separate areas both for ambient (room temperature) food or chilled food. This is used by the caterer not only to present the food but also to aid the self-service operation of the establishment. The chilled unit would be subject to the same procedures as a normal refrigerator. However, care must be taken as customers are picking up and putting down items that could raise the temperature of the food.

Waiter (or waitress) station

In a large restaurant or hotel, it is commonplace to see functional units to store items of crockery, cutlery and any other tableware for a particular area and staff to use.

Small equipment

Crockery

The crockery a caterer uses must be durable, dishwasher proof, and attractive. In some establishments, for example a gourmet restaurant, big, attractive, colourful plates are used to showcase particular dishes. Crockery that is chipped or damaged should be discarded as it may present a hygiene or safety risk.

Cutlery

Cutlery should be functional yet attractive. When taking cutlery out of the dishwasher, it should be polished immediately to avoid streaking. Customers are put off by dirty or streaky cutlery and it could affect the overall opinion of the establishment.

Tablecloths and napkins

Tablecloths and napkins are purchased or hired to match the décor within the restaurant or eating area. For example, a hotel may require champagne-coloured linen for a wedding function, whereas a café may require wipeable tablecloths for a busy weekend.

Table arrangements

These can take the form of candles, flower arrangements or even a bottle of olive oil filled with chillies and fresh herbs. For special occasions, such as Valentine's Day, chocolates may be put into a presentation box and wrapped with ribbon.

Themed materials

Special materials can be purchased or made to complement either special occasions or particular themes. For example, at Christmas the restaurant or dining area could be decorated with tinsel, mistletoe, and so on, but also customers might have a centrepiece on each table, a card and speciality crackers.

A themed setting is used for events such as Christmas

ACTIVITY

Find out 10 different occasions or events that could be hosted in a variety of catering environments.

Now choose one of the events and list the equipment needed to help the smooth running of the event.

CHECK YOUR KNOWLEDGE

1 What is a guéridon trolley and what is its use?
2 Name three different ways of making coffee.
3 What are the advantages to the caterer of a food display unit?

4.4 Use and maintenance of equipment

Use of equipment

As a general rule, you should always follow manufacturers instructions before using any item of equipment but here are a few guidelines:

- When using electrical equipment, always use guards.
- Report any damaged or faulty equipment.
- Avoid using items other than the plunger when mincing foodstuffs. For example, it has been reported that people have used wooden spoons, rolling pins or even fingers to push food through a mincing machine.
- Do not overload machinery. For example, too much dough in a mixing machine will overload the motor and cause a safety risk.
- Report bare wires or any other safety risk.
- Report any dangerous practice by other individuals.
- Do not put knives or any other sharp objects in the sink.

Maintenance and servicing

Regular maintenance of equipment is essential to the smooth running of a commercial kitchen. If machinery has not been maintained, it could be either unsafe or inefficient. In addition to this, it could break down. For example, a convection oven breaking down in the middle of a lunchtime service could be a disaster for the establishment. Routine safety checks should be made by a trained professional, highlighting any faults and ensuring safety for both employees and visiting customers.

Cleaning of equipment

As previously mentioned, a dishwasher can be used to clean both cutlery and crockery. It can also be used to clean a whole variety of bowls, whisks, and so on. Sometimes, hot soapy water is the only way to clean a pan properly, especially with ingrained dirt or a burned sauce.

Glassware requires special attention and should be either washed in a separate sink or in an industrial glass washer. Copper and silverware require special solutions or products for a shiny presentable finish.

Large equipment should be cleaned using the appropriate cleaning solution. However, take care when using a product such as an oven cleaner, when you should wear goggles, gloves, facemask and protective clothing.

Surfaces once cleaned should be sprayed or applied with an anti-bacterial solution to ensure effective food safety within that area.

Storage of cleaning materials

General cleaning materials, including oven cleaner, bleach and the majority of any other products, should be stored in a locked cupboard away from non-permitted staff and visiting customers. Cleaning materials should not be mixed and should be in separate containers to avoid either the risk of a chemical reaction or harm to an individual.

All bottles and products must be clearly identified and labelled correctly, ideally in the original packaging to avoid any misunderstanding and subsequent incident.

COSHH

COSHH (Control of Substances Hazardous to Health) is the training relating to the use, storage and application of chemical substances. This program of study features basic first aid, what you need to do in the event of an accident and the right way to carry out tasks.

There have been incidents where, for example, in a public house one employee was badly injured when mistaking pipe cleaning fluid for lemonade. It was in the wrong bottle and of a similar colour. COSHH procedures had not been followed and the public house was open to prosecution.

FIND OUT

Go to the COSHH website http://www.hse.gov.uk/catering/casestudies.htm and choose a case study. Summarise the information and answer the following questions:

1 What happened?

2 Who was to blame?

3 What were the implications for both the individuals involved and the establishment?

4 What would have prevented the incident?

Signs such as these are used to warn people

CHECK YOUR KNOWLEDGE

1 Why should you follow the manufacturer's guidelines when using large electrical equipment?

2 What clothing should be used when using an oven cleaner?

3 Why should cleaning materials be stored in a locked cupboard?

ExamCafé

Exam preparation

Revision checklist

Which exam	Content	What to revise?
All for catering	Small equipment	You need to know the different types of knives and their uses.
		You need to have an understanding of colour coding, for example chopping boards.
		You should have an awareness of different small electrical machines and understand their uses.
		You should know other general small equipment used to assist the caterer in their preparations.
All for catering	Large equipment	You should know the difference in quality between domestic and commercial catering equipment.
		You need to know what a bain-marie is and what it is used for.
		You need to know different specialist large equipment that would benefit a large catering kitchen.
All for catering	Food service equipment	You need to have an awareness of different types of food service equipment, including a flambé trolley.
		You should know the benefits of a food display unit to the caterer.
		You should understand other small equipment used for food service.
All for catering	Use and maintenance	You should understand certain rules relating to the correct use of equipment.
		You should know the difference between maintenance and servicing.
		You should have an understanding of COSHH and how it relates to the caterer.

Activities

This is a practical unit which is supported by theory. For each piece of equipment the selection, use, cleaning and maintenance should be considered. An awareness of hygiene and health and safety is important in this section.

Exam preparation

Use past exam questions to check your knowledge. Most of the questions are about your knowledge and will ask you to apply your understanding to selected questions. Some questions may relate to catering terminology.

Sample question

You are going to purchase a set of knives. What special features should you consider when making your purchase?

(4 marks)

Examiner's tip

Think of chefs' knives rather than the knives you might use at home. For example, not every household would have a boning knife or a fish-filleting knife.

Sample answer

Special features to consider when purchasing knifes are:

- Weight of knife and balance
- Known brand
- Stainless steel, which is known for not rusting
- Wooden handles for ease of use
- Plastic handles which can go in the dishwasher and are more hygienic than wood
- Range of sizes, for example cooks knife and utility knife
- Whether the knife can hold an edge (stay sharp)

Sample question

Using a deep fat fryer can be dangerous. List three safety points when using this piece of equipment.

(3 marks)

Examiner's tip

Practical experience of using a deep fat fryer would help you to answer this type of question.

Sample answer

Safety points when using a deep fat fryer include:

- Do not throw food, or any other items, into the fryer – lower the food in carefully.
- Choose the correct temperature when cooking.
- Avoid water of any other liquids near the hot fat.
- Don't overload the fryer.
- Do not use wooden or plastic utensils to remove food items.

5.1 Environmental considerations

If everybody in the world lived as we do in the UK today, we would need three planets to sustain us. Looking after the environment and thinking about the sustainability of business activities is very important to help prevent global warming so that future generations have a world to live in.

Environmental policy

More and more hospitality establishments are deciding that sustainability is a key issue in their activities. Many establishments have produced an environmental policy for their organisation such as the one shown here, stating how they try to be sustainable.

The Six R's

There are six R's that are used when talking about sustainability and environmental issues:

- reduce
- reuse
- recycle
- rethink
- refuse
- repair.

These wil be covered over the next three chapters.

Some of the six R's have more relevance to the hospitality industry than others but they all need to be considered.

At this time in world history we believe that as a business we have a responsibility not only to minimise our impact but also to make environmental policy a key and integral part of our business strategy. For us this translates in to three main areas of action and planning.

On an immediate level we are committed to day-to-day policy which will minimise our environmental impact. Examples would be that we recycle glass, tin and cardboard and that we use energy saving bulbs wherever possible.

In the medium term we are implementing strategies which we see as over and above the basic day-to-day policies. Examples of these strategies would be the recent setting up of our own facility to recycle used cooking oil into bio-diesel. Also, in the winter of 2007 we replaced all of our sunlounge windows with double glazed units.

We are also looking at the long term. For us this involves looking at ways in which we can run the hotel using an increasing amount of renewable energy sources. We have started investigations into heating our water through solar panelling and we are watching the developments in wind energy with interest.

St Columba Hotel
Isle of Iona, Argyll, Scotland, PA76 6SL

Reduce

Reduce is about minimising the amount of materials and energy that is used to make a product or for an activity.

'One of the biggest household guzzlers is the very thing few of us could countenance life without: the kettle. The energy used to boil one kettle of water could light a room for an entire evening. On top of that, most of us heat more water than we need.' (BBC)

How many hotel rooms now have tea and coffee-making facilities? What size kettle do they use? Is it essential to have this facility in the room? Is room service with free tea and coffee a solution? What would the cost in wages be for this?

Reducing for the hospitality industry means reducing water and energy:

Water

- Only have showers in the bathroom as showers use less than half of the amount of water as baths.

- Reduce the amount of washing done. Don't change sheets for customers staying more than one night. Don't change towels everyday.

Energy

- Reduce the temperature in the public areas by 1 °C.
- Turn off lights, televisions and heating in bedrooms until occupied.
- Use keycards that have to be placed in electronic boxes to activate electricity.
- Use economic energy sources in the kitchen such as halogen hobs.

Unhealthy food

In the broader sense of sustainability, reduce can also mean reduce the amount of fat, sugar and salt in dishes as too many of these can cause heart disease, diabetes, osteoporosis, diverticulitis, appendicitis and some cancers. This causes pressure on the health service and cannot be sustainable for the long-term. Also, processed foods are the foods that contain too much fat, sugar and salt. Processed foods have a high impact on the planet compared to unprocessed foods because they are manufactured using energy and water. The hospitality industry can help by using fewer processed foods and producing healthy dishes.

Reuse

Reuse is about taking an existing product that has become waste and using it for another purpose, without processing it.

'Britain throws away £20 billion worth of unused food every year – equal to five times our spending on international aid and enough to lift 150 million people out of starvation.' (The Independent 15.03.05)

When food waste ends up in a landfill site, it rots and produces ethane, a powerful greenhouse gas.

Food is far more difficult to reuse than other materials such as fabric but it does need to be reused. For example, leftover roast meat could be used to make a cottage pie for staff. Leftover chicken can be made into a curry. Leftover vegetables can be made into a minestrone soup. A lot of traditional ways with leftover foods have been lost in today's world, but could be revived.

One way to make sure that the amount of food to reuse is reduced is to reduce portion sizes or have a choice of portion sizes in a menu so the customer decides how hungry they are. 'Light bites' and a choice of large or small portions of pasta or size of pizza are already used to address food wastage.

Reuse can also mean to reuse towels more than once. This saves energy and water. Most bathrooms now have a sign asking guests to hang the towel on the rail if they want to reuse it and leave it on the floor if they would like it washed.

ACTIVITY

Analyse the sustainability of a hospitality establishment you have visited. Think particularly about how they are reducing and reusing.

CHECK YOUR KNOWLEDGE

1 What are the six R's?
2 How much energy does a kettle use?
3 How much waste food is thrown away each year?
4 Why is not washing hotel towels environmentally friendly?

5.2 Recycle

Recycling is when an existing waste product is reprocessed into a new product. It is the most well-known way for people to understand the term environmentally friendly but is only a small part of sustainability. This is partly because recycling requires transportation and reprocessing, both of which use energy. Every 10 per cent more we recycle, we only reduce our eco-footprint by 1 per cent. Recycling is important, however, and we should continue to increase our recycling efforts.

Food packaging

Food packaging accounts for more than 60 per cent of the total packaging used in this country. We do need to use packaging for food as it:

- holds and contains the contents – especially liquids
- makes it last longer – keeps it fresh – therefore reducing wastage
- makes it easier to transport, handle and serve – protects from physical damage
- makes it hygienic – protects from contamination
- makes it attractive to buy – because of the packaging design
- gives information about the contents including when to eat it
- is used when the food is reheated.

Types of packaging

There are four main types of packaging: glass, paper or card, metal, plastic. All of them have advantages and disadvantages:

Packaging type	Advantages	Disadvantages
Glass	• reusable – can be sealed • strong • recyclable • can be printed on	• breakable • heavy
Paper or card	• made from a sustainable source – trees • can be recycled • lightweight • can be strong – when dry • very easy to print on	• crushes easily • weak when wet • recycled card and paper • cannot be used for food because of impurities in it
Metal	• strong • rigid • recyclable • can be printed on	• expensive – uses a valuable resource extracted from the ground • reacts with food unless coated inside • cannot use in microwave
Plastic	• strong • flexible – easy to shape • easily printed • does not react with food	• unsustainable resource – made from oil • not always easy to recycle • so many different types of plastic

Different needs

Different foods need to be packaged with different materials, depending on who buys it and how it will be used.

- Glass bottles are best to use in pubs and bars – individual portions and easy to collect and recycle.
- Cans are best if you are on the move. A can is lightweight and can be put in special can collection points.
- Plastic bottles mean that you can open the bottle again and again. This is economic for large amounts, but can be heavy.

Mixed-material packaging

More than half of all packaging is plastic, made from a non-renewable resource and the most difficult to recycle. But there is also mixed-material packaging such as Tetra Pak or Gualapack, where recycling is even more difficult.

Tetra Pak is made up of 70 per cent paperboard, 24 per cent LDPE – a plastic, and 6 per cent aluminium. It has been suggested that Tetra Paks can stop light depleting the vitamins and minerals in drinks – compared to glass or plastic packaging, and that the packaging is good for the environment because the paperboard is made from a renewable resource. At the moment, there is only one recycling plant in the UK for Tetra Pak cartons. On average, each UK household used 2.3 kg of Tetra Pak cartons a year.

Biodegradable packaging

There has been a lot of development with **biodegradable** packaging for disposable products, as well as general food packaging.

Corn starch is composted back to soil in 12 weeks. It is made into a 'bio-bottle' and is used for bottled water and smoothies. The caps are as yet not biodegradable.

Potato pack is an alternative to polystyrene and can be used for takeaway food as well as disposable plates and cups and packaging for fruit and vegetables. It biodegrades within weeks.

KEY TERM

Biodegradable: capable of decaying through the action of living organisms.

ACTIVITY

Compare the packaging used between two sandwich outlets such as Subway and Eat or Prêt à manger. Which uses the most sustainable packaging and why?

CHECK YOUR KNOWLEDGE

1 Why do we need food packaging?
2 What packaging is recyclable?
3 What packaging is made from renewable resources?
4 What is the disadvantage of mixed-material packaging?
5 What does biodegradable mean?

5.3 More environmental considerations

Reduce, reuse and recycle are the three most well-known of the six R's. But it is worthwhile considering the other three (rethink, refuse and repair) so that every aspect of sustainability – consideration to the environment has been covered.

Rethink

Rethink is about rethinking our current lifestyles and the way we design and make things. For the hospitality industry, this can be wide-reaching:

- Rethink how new hospitality buildings are made: the materials used to build them, the energy source – such as underground heating or a wind turbine. It is also about the overall design of the building so that it uses as much natural light and as little heating as possible.

- Rethink about existing buildings and how they can become more energy efficient – double glazing, loft insulation, ventilation, air conditioning.

- Rethink cooking methods so that menu items use up less energy – for example, have more 'one pot' dishes such as cassoulet, on a menu.

- Rethink the ingredients used in dishes so that seasonal local foods are used, which use less **food miles**. Food miles is a term which refers to the distance food is transported from the time of its production until it reaches the consumer. It is one dimension used in assessing the environmental impact of food.

- Rethink the use of throwaway cups for coffee and tea. Cafes and coffee shops could offer to put drink in a cup you provide at a reduced cost to encourage customers – a bit like the carrier bag situation in supermarkets. This is already being done in universities in Canada and Germany where students are given a reusable cup and pay much less for drinks if they use it!

KEY TERM

Food miles: a calculation of the distance food travels from its place of origin or production to the consumer.

CASE STUDY

Youth Hostel Association (YHA) Langdon Beck is a 30-bed youth hostel – set in a stunning but very exposed location 1,300 feet up in the wild North Pennines at Forest in Teesdale, County Durham. A range of energy conservation and carbon reducing features has been used which has helped to achieve a 50% cut in total energy consumption. This range of energy conservation and carbon reducing features – includes:

- Sheep's wool loft insulation and cavity wall insulation
- Fully double glazed windows
- Replacement of open coal fire with wood burning stove
- Solar hot water panels
- 2.5kW wind turbine
- 2.4kW solar PV system.

A total of 60% of electricity is now generated on site, and the remainder is purchased from renewable providers. A key part of the work here has been in customer communication and education. The use of 'Good Guest Cards' encourages visitors to use energy more efficiently, and there are rigorous daily management routines relating to energy management and monitoring.

- This YHA is an ecoflower establishment. What energy conservation method do you think saved the most energy?

Refuse

Refuse leads on from rethinking our lifestyles and is about not accepting a product or service if you don't need it or if it is environmentally or socially unsustainable. Food is the largest single factor affecting our eco-footprint. Packaging, processing and transport use huge amounts of energy.

Hospitality establishments can:

- refuse to use GM – (genetically modified foods) or foods produced using child labour or where the workers have been paid unfair wages
- choose to use Fair Trade and organic foods
- refuse to use food that use lots of food miles, such as asparagus flown in from Peru six months of the year
- choose to use local seasonal foods
- refuse to use highly packaged foods
- choose to use loose fruit and vegetables and sacks of rice and flour.

Repair

Repair is about when a product breaks down or doesn't function properly. You fix it rather than throw it away. It's about asking, is new best? And are new items just for fashion sustainable?

For the hospitality industry, this means:

- having a policy to try and repair damaged or faulty kitchen equipment
- having a policy of maintenance of the building that will help sustain it for longer rather than renew it all (for example, reupholstering existing chairs and settees rather than buying new ones).

If the hospitality industry considers the six R's, they will consider the environmental and social issues necessary to make their operation sustainable.

CHECK YOUR KNOWLEDGE

1 What types of foods should establishments refuse to use if they want to be sustainable?

2 What type of foods should they use if they want to be sustainable?

3 What is an ecoflower establishment?

ACTIVITY

Write an environmental policy for an establishment you have visited. Make sure that you include points about all six R's.

MENU

MAIN COURSES

Three Fishes Pie, (Fleetwood) Fish & Seawater Prawns baked with Mashed Potato, sprinkled with Mrs Kirkham's (Lancashire) Cheese £9.95

Battered Deep Fried Haddock, Marrowfat Peas, Real Chips in Dripping, Tartare Sauce £11.95

North Sea Cod Fish Cakes, Curly Leaf Parsley Sauce, Spring Cabbage £9.00

Heather Reared (Bowland Lamb) Lancashire Hotpot, Pickled Red Cabbage £10.50

(V) (Leagram's) Organic Creamy, Curd Cheese & Onion Pie, Short Crust Pastry, Sour Cream Jackets, Plum Tomato Salad £10.50

New Season's (Bowland) Lamb's Liver, Confit Kidney, (Foragers') Streaky Bacon, Spring Onions, Parsely Potato Cake £9.50

Gloucester Old Spot Sausages, Mash, White Onion Sauce £8.50

(V) Flan of (Ascroft's) Cauliflower and Organic Sheeps' Milk Curd Cheese, Roast Beetroot Salad £8.50

DESSERTS

Local Strawberries, Clotted Cream and Meringue £5.00

Vanilla Junket, Raspberries, (Goosnargh Cakes) £5.00

Old English Sherry Trifle £4.50

Elderflower Syllabub & Jelly, (Crushed Grasmere Ginger) Bread £4.50

The Three Fishes restaurant at Mitton in Lancashire prides itself on locally sourced ingredients.

Exam**Café**

Revision checklist

Which exam:	Content	What to revise
BOTH	Environmental considerations	You need to know what an environmental policy includes and what the six R's are and mean. You need to know how the industry reduces and reuses.
Mostly CAT but some HOS	Recycling and packaging	You need to know about different types of food packaging and what material is best for what need. You also need to know how to recycle them.
Mostly HOS but some CAT	More environmental considerations	You need to know how the industry can reduce, rethink, refuse and repair.

Activities

Mindmap the six R's and make sure that you can give several examples of how the industry can follow these.

Exam preparation

Sample question

1 The hospitality and catering industry produce a lot of waste. It is important that they help protect the environment by reducing the amount of waste produced.
   a Suggest three ways in which kitchen staff can reduce waste   (3 marks)
   b Describe ways in which a hotel can reduce, reuse and recycle products   (4 marks)
   c Discuss how a hotel can encourage guests to help protect the environment   (6 marks)

Sample answer

a Training of staff to prepare food correctly including the right portion size.
Recycling packaging.
Buying food in bulk so there is less packaging.

b Recycling waste from the kitchen – compost to use in gardens, paper, plastic bottles.
Reduce packaging – on soaps etc., on food ingredients – buy in bulk or unpackaged vegetables. Not putting fresh toilet rolls out for each guest, refillable bottles of shower gel. Light sensors and electricity keys for rooms. Re-use towels and sheets by not changing them everyday.

c Leave a copy of the environmental policy out in the room for guests to read that highlights things like temperature controls and lighting. Leave notices about reusing towels, turning off lights and using showers. Supplying some things at reception rather than in each room, such as a mending kit and some toiletries so that it encourages own use.
Identifying menu items that have been locally sourced. Having recycling bins everywhere.

Examiner says:
Careful reading of this question is necessary:

The first part is about reducing only.

The second part is about three R's. You must make sure that you cover all of the three in this type of answer.

The third part is quite specific asking for ideas for guests not workers.

2 Discuss the range of packaging materials suitable for wrapping hot and cold sandwiches. (6 marks)

Sample answer

Cold sandwiches are best served in hinged plastic boxes. If these are triangular it means that you can see the filling. The box means that you can see the sandwich and that it will not be squashed. It is a sealed box so it protects the sandwich from bacteria.

Other possible packaging is a paper bag or waxed paper bag or cellophane top or even a cardboard box. These all have disadvantages, such as less protection or easily squashed.

For a hot sandwich the best packaging is a polystyrene box as this not only protects from squashing but it also keeps it warm.

Examiner says:
This type of question needs planning. Discussion means looking at advantages and disadvantages so to get full marks, both of these need mentioning, as well as packaging for hot as well as cold sandwiches.

Planning and structuring an answer

All questions worth four or more marks should be approached as if you were writing a mini-essay. Planning should happen before you write an answer. These questions get full-marks when answers are 'well written and detailed'. This means well-structured. A well-structured answer is like an essay and has an introduction and a conclusion (or end) to it.

Chapter 6

COMMUNICATION AND TEAMWORK

6.1 The importance of effective teamwork

In the hospitality and catering industry, it is usual to work as a member of a team. One chef cannot cook all the dinners, one room attendant cannot clean all the rooms and one waiter cannot serve all the guests.

Teamwork

The industry relies heavily on teamwork. This is essential within departments, such as between the kitchen and house-keeping, but also across different departments. For example:

- Reception staff need housekeeping staff to tell them when rooms are ready.
- Housekeeping staff need the reception team to let them know when customers have checked out so that they can clean the room.
- Restaurant staff need the chef to tell them whether any food has run out and when food is ready to serve.
- The kitchen staff need the banqueting manager to tell them when to dish up the next course.
- The kitchen staff need the reception team to tell them how many people are booked into the hotel so that they can begin their preparation.

What is a team?

A team is a group of individuals working together towards a clearly defined goal or objective.

So a restaurant team has a goal of serving all guests safely and systematically so that the best customer satisfaction is achieved.

A housekeeping team has a goal to clean all the rooms to a specific standard as quickly as possible.

Teams work best if all members are committed to the job and have the resources to do it properly. The team must also be open and democratic so all ideas and concerns can be shared by its members. It also needs the support of senior management within the organisation.

Teamwork is important at all levels of the industry

All teams need a team leader. The success of a team depends on this person. They:

- decide who works in the team – a head chef interviews and employs kitchen staff – not the hotel manager
- decide what the team has to do – divide up the work – a restaurant manager allocates sections of the room to different staff
- take responsibility for the standard of work produced – a head chef usually checks every meal sent out of the kitchen
- make sure that the task is carried out safely – that rules – and the law – are kept to.

A team leader must:

- set a good example
- be respected by all the team members
- be consistent in decisions made
- encourage, motivate and support team members.

The benefits of teamwork

The two most important benefits of working in a team are that more gets done, and because of that, there is better customer service.

Other benefits are:

- a higher output of work – achieved for less effort
- a happier workforce – people are usually happier working in a group
- increased loyalty – gives a feeling of worth and improves the desire to give good customer service (also likely to reduce absenteeism)
- less staff conflict – because responsibility for work and decisions is shared
- a more creative workforce as a happy team member is likely to come forward with ideas to improve work practices and reduce costs or increase efficiency
- increased sales – a teamwork approach is likely to increase sales, for example, if the team has a target of selling 50 portions of onion rings for a night – all the team work towards this and help each other.

Working as a team member also has advantages such as:

- feeling more valued at work
- being able to learn from others – e.g. a commis chef will learn from a pastry chef
- being able to share knowledge, e.g. one waiter showing another a different napkin fold
- greater job satisfaction
- having the support of others
- benefiting from team 'perks', such as a productivity bonus.

A team leader has an important role in training

ACTIVITY

Write about a team you have worked in. Think about the benefits of this teamwork. What did you learn?

CHECK YOUR KNOWLEDGE

1 What is teamwork?

2 What does a team leader do?

3 What skills will a team leader have?

4 Why is a team workforce likely to be more creative?

6.2 How teams work

Teamwork means working effectively together with other staff. It could be a small group of three staff working in a team, or a larger group of ten or more staff. Whether the team is small or large, the qualities of a good team member will be the same.

Team members will be willing to:

- communicate effectively with others
- respect other team members
- develop a sense of comradeship with others in the team
- be helpful towards team members
- be aware of other team members' limitations
- be reliable and punctual
- develop a selfless attitude
- delight in others' success
- demonstrate a sense of humour in a crisis
- give praise and encouragement to other team members
- be honest and open with other team members
- listen to other team members
- take responsibility for designating tasks.

Stages in teamwork

Teams go through several stages before they begin to achieve an excellent level of performance:

Stage 1: Forming

When a team is given a task, it is important that each member is sure what the task is and how best to achieve the end result. They will also need to know what resources they need, what extra information they will need to help them with the task, and what research they might have to do.

Stage 2: Storming

Many teams go through a stage of disruption and disagreement. This is likely to happen when new ideas are challenged and discussed. If the team survives this, there will be more trust.

Stage 3: Norming

This is when a team starts to operate as one unit, rather than a number of individuals trying to impose their ideas and get their own way.

Stage 4: Performing

This is when the team works really well together because they have gone through the previous stages. This is when the highest level of performance is achieved.

Good teamwork

So good teamwork can be recognised when:

- team members communicate – talk to each other – effectively
- team members feel able to suggest ideas
- team members know what is expected of them
- team members share responsibility to make sure tasks are done
- tasks are carried out quickly and efficiently
- team members are happy and have high self-esteem.

Ultimately, you can recognise a good team when work is efficient and high customer satisfaction is achieved.

What affects team behaviour?

Some teams do not work efficiently. There can be a number of reasons for this, such as:

- the attitude and behaviour of the team leader
- members not carrying out their fair share of the workload

Which team member is not pulling their weight?

- different social skills of team members, including cultural differences
- strong personalities who want to dominate the team, which can then cause conflict or personality clashes
- stress and pressure when carrying out the task.

CASE STUDY

Bernadette was a manager of the school canteen. She had eight kitchen assistants who came into work at 9am and were each responsible for making two dishes on the menu that day. They often complained about how their colleagues worked, that they were too slow and that they always had to wait to use equipment, such as food mixers and ovens. Some staff finished their two dishes quickly and did not want to help others. Some staff complained about the flavour and presentation of the dishes they had not made.

Bernadette decided to create two teams of assistants who worked each day on the main dishes or the desserts and vegetables. This meant that the staff had to work together and help each other more. They organised the use of equipment better and stopped criticising each other's dishes. They were more efficient which meant they had more time for presentation and discussions on ways to improve things. They became happier in their jobs and the food improved.

- If there were four chefs making pizzas in a restaurant, how could the team leader divide the work up to create an efficient and happy team?

TRY THIS

First, work as individuals and all produce a batch of biscuits. Secondly, work as a team of four or more. Produce biscuits in this team. Evaluate the quality and quantity of the biscuits made in each case, and the time it took to make them.

CHECK YOUR KNOWLEDGE

1 Describe the stages of teamwork that are forming, storming, norming and performing.

2 List reasons why some teams don't work.

6.3 The importance of communication skills and written communication

Have you ever been in a situation where you thought 'What did he say?' or 'What did she mean?' Have you ever read a diagram or instruction and thought 'I don't understand this' or 'This isn't explained well'. If you have, you have experienced poor communication.

External communication

Effective communication skills are essential in the hospitality and catering industry. Good communication is a key aspect of good customer service in all activities in the industry. This is called external communication.

Communication is important both when facing customers and dealing with colleagues

External communication is carried out in many forms:

* verbal – speaking and listening
* non-verbal – body language – expressions, gestures, posture, eye contact
* written – on paper or using ICT.

Internal communication

Communication is a two-way process with responsibilities on both sides. It is also essential for effective teamwork. This is internal communication. How the team you work in and your other colleagues communicate with each other will impact on the quality of service you provide. You need to communicate by:

* Telling colleagues what is required – for example, writing down orders in a clear, easy-to-read way so no mistakes are made.
* Seeking information – from more experienced or senior members of staff. This may be written or spoken.
* NOT being over familiar with colleagues if it is likely that customers can overhear. A certain amount of formality is needed in work situations.

Urgent and non-urgent

Communication can be urgent or non-urgent, which influences how and by what method you communicate. For example, this could be the difference between dealing with a complaint or making 'small talk' (chatting) with customers. Dealing with urgent communication can be difficult if it involves an upset or distressed customer. It is important to stay calm in these situations and seek help from senior staff.

Effective letter-writing needs the following three basic principles:

- the need to define the purpose of the letter
- the need always to consider the reader of the letter
- the need always to use language appropriate for these two above points.

Also important are:

- Be clear – use the right punctuation.
- Be concise – don't 'pad it out'.
- Be correct – with facts and figures and spelling and grammar.
- Be complete – provide all information needed.

- Be courteous – use the right words to create the right tone.
- Make sure that the layout is neat and attractive.
- Avoid use of jargon.

Letters need to fall into three parts:
1 context – what it is about
2 detail – the facts
3 conclusion.

Written communication

There are many forms of written communication used in the hospitality and catering industry. The main ones are letter-writing, faxes, memos and record or work cards. There are also menus to write and place cards and signs to draw and write.

This written communication can be paper or ICT-based.

Take care in what you want to say as once the communication has been sent, you can't influence how others interpret it and have no chance to change the tone. Something that is badly written with incorrect spelling or bad grammar gives a bad impression.

Fax

This is a written form of communication sent through the telephone network by a special machine.

This form of communication can be an instant sending of a letter or documentation. Faxes are not very common now because of the increased use of emails but they can be useful occasionally.

Email

This is another instant form of communication and has the advantage of being able to send large documents without feeding each page through a fax machine. Often letters sent by email are less formal than paper letters for example 'regards' is often used at the end of an email letter rather than 'yours sincerely' at the end of a paper letter. Memos are also sent via email. Emails are used internally – especially for memos, as well as externally to send promotional offers and confirmation of bookings, as well as personal letters.

Memos

These are still used for internal communication and can be used as reminders of meetings or to pass down facts or information from a manager or supervisor. The contents are short and concise.

ACTIVITY

Write a letter to a butcher supplier complaining about the size of the chicken breasts delivered the week before. Be polite but express your concern.

CHECK YOUR KNOWLEDGE

1 List the three types of communication.
2 Give two examples of urgent communication and two of non-urgent communication.
3 What are the three parts of a letter?

6.4 Types of communication – verbal and non-verbal

Verbal communication is probably the most important way of communicating in the industry. A lot can be conveyed in a voice. The volume, tone, pitch and pace of your voice is important, whether you speak quietly or loudly, whether you change the tone during speaking, and whether you make gestures during speaking, such as sighs and laughter.

There are two main types of verbal communication: face-to-face and by telephone:

Face-to-face

This communication has many advantages over other forms of communication because:

- You can observe the customer and get an idea of how they are feeling.
- You can use non-verbal communication including personal presentation and hygiene to support what you are saying.
- You can use your personality to build a rapport with customers.
- It is easier to find out exactly what a customer wants when you can see their reaction to suggestions.

When communicating with customers:

- Remember that first impressions count.
- Smile.
- Be smart and clean with good personal hygiene, and have good posture.
- Use body language to show interest.
- Maintain eye contact.
- Practice the art of active listening – identify the main items and then respond and take action.
- Gather more information using open questions – ones that do not just require yes and no answers.
- Use the person's name to show recognition and friendliness.
- Provide solutions.

On the telephone

The only thing that will create an impression on the telephone is your voice. It is important to remember that the impression you make comes from the words you use and the tone and pitch of your voice. When answering the phone:

A good telephone manner is important for business

- Answer promptly – within three or four rings (or apologise for the delay).
- Greet the caller and identify your establishment, the department and yourself. Many establishments have a set way that the phone must be answered.
- Offer help – 'How can I help you?'
- Sound confident and pleasant – smile while you talk – this is transferred to your voice.
- Speak clearly.
- Listen.
- Make notes including who the caller is and contact details.
- Confirm details by repeating the main points.
- Give the caller the opportunity to ask more questions by asking if there is anything else you can help with.
- Thank the caller and say goodbye.
- Carry out what you need to do immediately.

If you are making a call, the reverse is required. You need to be clear about the purpose of the call, who you want to speak to and what information you need. Make notes during the call and carry out any follow-up action as soon as possible.

Non-verbal communication

This type of communication gives a lot of information about others and ourselves, without even speaking. Non-verbal communication is the ability to convey information and feelings through the use of body language.

It includes:
- facial expressions – smiles, frowns, narrowed eyes, eyes to the ceiling, friendliness, boredom, anger
- gestures – thumbs-up signs, pointing fingers, head nods, shaking of the head showing disagreement, focus
- movements – pacing up and down, finger drumming, strolling, impatience, transmitting anxiety
- physical contact – shaking hands – firm or feeble, prodding with forefinger, slapping on the back, transmitting greeting or insistence
- positioning – keeping a respectful distance, looking over someone's shoulder, sitting close to someone, transmitting awareness of different status
- posture – standing up straight, lounging, sitting hunched up, leaning forward, spreading out on a chair, transmitting alertness, nervousness
- eye contact – steady contact, downcast, flitting around, vacant.

It is important to be aware of this type of communication as it accounts for over half of what comes across in any situation.

6.5 Record-keeping

Record-keeping is a vital part of the hospitality industry. The restaurant needs to know how many people are booked that night, when they are arriving, how many they are and what at least one of them is called. The conference centre needs to know the type of lunch an organisation has ordered and whether anyone has a special diet that needs considering. A hostel needs to know how many rooms are left to sell on a particular day. The only way they know is to look at records of bookings and information recorded about that booking.

Records also help inform a business when analysing its sales and working out how to improve and develop.

Records are made of staff rotas, room bookings, accounts, invoices, room management, event and function bookings, orders and stock control. Most records are now computerised.

Databases, spreadsheets and word documents are used, depending on the type of record required.

Examples of record-keeping

- reservation system for bedrooms and conference rooms and restaurants
- arrival and departure lists – or a room status report
- standard letters compiled
- reports and summaries, including analysis of turnover, sales projection figures and daily analysis of sales
- telephone logging
- guests' accounts constantly updated
- billing for guests' services, such as early morning newspapers
- charging for food and beverage services
- financial statistics
- nightly audit statistics
- enquiry records
- control of stock
- guest history cards.

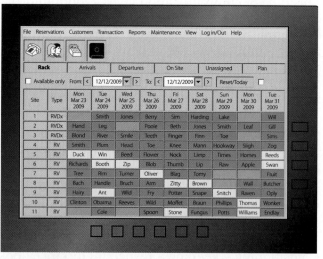

Record-keeping systems keep a full record of on-going issues in the businesss

A lot of this information recorded needs to be communicated between people and departments. It is important that the easiest and most efficient methods are used to store and communicate this information.

Record cards

Record cards are used to record facts in all sections of the hospitality and catering industry. These might be as a database or a paper filing system that is indexed and kept in chronological order so that the information is easily accessed. Some examples are below:

Record cards such as these are used throughout the hospitality industry

Reception/front office:
- guest history cards
- registration cards
- previous guests' names and addresses
- emergency contactors' names and addresses.

Kitchen:
- recipes
- equipment maintenance records
- HACCP systems including cleaning routines for equipment
- suppliers' names and addresses.

Housekeeping:
- room redecoration records
- equipment maintenance records
- linen repair records
- suppliers' names and addresses.

Personnel:
- staff clocking-in cards
- staff names and addresses
- emergency medical call out cards.

Surname			Initial		Title	Room #
Home Address				Company/Convention		
City	State	P/Code				
Phone No				Car Registration		

Method Of Payment
- ☐ Bankcard ☐ MasterCard
- ☐ Visa ☐ Cash
- ☐ Amex ☐ Diners Club

By Prior Arrangement
- ☐ Company Charge
- ☐ Cheque

The hotel assumes no responsibility for loss of money or other valuables. We are not responsible for articles left in the room or automobiles. A safe is provided for the deposit of valuables.
Every person signing this document and/or actually occupying or utilizing services shall be personally liable for all accommodation, restaurant and other charges in addition to the customers named in the agreement and even if the account is sent in the first instance to that customer or company.
Signature   Signature

OFFICE USE ONLY	Account #	Rate	Arrival	Departure
	Type	A/C	Arrival Time	GSA

The 1998 Data Protection Act

This act was passed by parliament to control the way information is handled and to give legal rights to people who have information recorded about them.

The Data Protection Act was developed to give protection and lay down rules about how data about people can be used. Usually this data is stored on a computer.

Some data and information stored on computer disks is personal and needs to be kept confidential. People want to keep their details away from the view of just anybody. The Data Protection Act sets up rules to prevent unauthorised access to personal data and information.

So, the Act covers:

- information or data stored on a computer or an organised paper filing system about living people.

The Act works:

- by setting up rules that people have to follow
- having an Information Commissioner to enforce the rules.

It does not stop companies storing information about people. It just makes them follow rules in how they do so.

Design a record sheet that logs details of anyone who phones up enquiring about staying at a hotel. List the information you would like to get from these callers.

CHECK YOUR KNOWLEDGE

1 Why is record-keeping vital for the hospitality industry?
2 How can record cards be useful for the housekeeping department?
3 Explain briefly what the data protection act does.

ExamCafé

Revision checklist

Which exam	Content	What to revise
HOS and CAT	The importance of teamwork	You need to understand why teams are important in the hospitality industry and the benefits of teamwork. You need to know what a team is and the skills needed in a team leader.
HOS and CAT	How teams work	You need to be able to recognise what is required in a team member and the stages a team will go through until it works successfully. You need to be able to recognise what can stop a team working well.
HOS and CAT	The importance of communication skills and written communication	You need to know about external and internal communication and about the different types of written communication.
HOS and CAT	Types of communication	You need to know face-to-face and telephone communication are both verbal communication and how they are different. You need to understand the importance of non-verbal communication.
HOS and CAT	Record-keeping	You need to know about all the different types of record-keeping and the Data Protection Act.
HOS and CAT	Stock control and billing	You need to know what a good stock control system is and about the purchasing cycle. You also need to know how customers are billed and how VAT affects this bill.

Common mistakes

The same answer is repeated in a different way, such as people must get on with each other and they must not fall out with each other – is really the same point.

Activities

Think about different teams in the industry and how they improve service. Work out how to communicate with who and why.

Exam preparation

Some knowledge needs to be learnt for this unit but again practical experience of working in teams will give you examples that could be used in exam answers.

Sample question

1 a Give three reasons why teamwork is important when working in a restaurant.
  b Identify three problems that may occur if the reception staff did not communicate with the housekeeping staff.

Sample answer

a It saves time as jobs get done faster. Someone can see if another worker for example the chef in charge of desserts could be really busy at a time when the chef serving starters is quiet. They can help each other.

Teamwork also means that everyone tells everyone else what is happening or about things such as the menu choice. That means better service.

b They would not know what rooms to clean, who was staying on another day so did not need the beds changing and also later on in the day, what rooms are ready for occupancy.

---

2 It is important for staff in the hospitality and catering industry to keep records.
   a State the type of record-keeping used for the following:
       i checking food stuffs into a kitchen store
       ii to find how many people are planning to eat in the restaurant
       iii checking how many people are staying in the hotel
   b Why is stock control important in a busy kitchen?

Sample answer

a i   stock control sheet/ stock records/ order book/ delivery note
   ii   restaurant booking form
   iii booking reference that shows rooms taken – check computer bookings

b So that they know what to order and what foods that are available to cook with. So that there is less waste which means more profit.

Chapter 7

MENU PLANNING

7.1 Nutrition and healthy eating

Catering terminology:

- à la carte – individually priced dishes on a menu
- menu – a list of available dishes
- table d'hote – a fixed price menu with limited choice

Nutrients

Carbohydrates

These are split into two main categories: complex and simple. Simple carbohydrates can either be the natural sugars found in fruits and vegetables, or the processed sugars found in chocolate, cakes, pastries, biscuits and even pizza. The complex carbohydrates or starchy foods are found naturally in foods but can be refined in processed foods. Examples of these include chickpeas, parsnips, root vegetables and wholemeal bread. Carbohydrate is a high-energy source and is readily converted into glucose and used by the body for energy.

Foods heavy in carbohydrates

Fats

Fats are broken down into saturated and unsaturated fat. The saturated fats include butter, lard and dripping. Unsaturated fats include olive oil, groundnut oil, sunflower oil and sesame oil. The Food Standards Agency (FSA) is trying to encourage individuals within the UK to eat less highly saturated fats and replace them with both unsaturated and also fats high in **Omega 3** found in oily fish. Make sure that you understand that the body does need fat. It is an essential source of energy, vitamins and fatty acids.

Foods heavy in fat

Protein

Protein is an essential nutrient important to your health, needed for the growth of the body and overall repair. Examples of animal proteins include meat, fish, cheese and eggs. Vegetable proteins include soya, rice, cereals, peas, beans and nuts. High-protein foods are used by athletes and body builders to develop muscle mass.

> **KEY TERM**
>
> **Omega 3:** a fatty acid which has been proven to reduce heart disease.

Vitamins

Vitamins are obtained in our diet and are not made by our bodies. They can either be fat or water soluble.

Fat-soluble vitamins

Vitamin A
Helps eye sight, skin growth and overall health.
Sources: liver, eggs and green vegetables.

Vitamin D
Promotes strong bones and teeth and any deficiency leads to rickets.
Sources: dairy produce, oils and fish.

Vitamin E
Promotes the growth of the body and helps the development of red blood cells.
Sources: nuts, wheatgerm, vegetable oils and cereals.

Water-soluble

Vitamin B1 (thiamine)

Helps break down carbohydrates into glucose.
Sources: cereals, red meat, egg yolk and nuts.

Vitamin B2 (riboflavin)

Good for general growth of the body and breakdown of protein and fat in addition to carbohydrates.
Sources: leafy green vegetables, fish and dairy produce.

Vitamin B12

Helps formation of red blood cells.
Sources: meat, fish and dairy produce.

Vitamin C

Protects from viruses, increases immunity via the body's defence system, helps keep skin, bones and muscles in good condition.
Sources: carrots, citrus fruit, peppers, potatoes and tomatoes.

Minerals

These are essential nutrients needed to keep bodily functions working properly. Minerals are broken down into both essential minerals and trace elements, for example, calcium and iron are classed as essential whereas zinc and iodine are classed as trace elements.

Calcium

This forms the skeletal structure of the body including bones and teeth. Calcium is present in a wide variety of foods including dairy produce, tofu, dried fruit and leafy green vegetables.

Iron

Iron is essential to the body for the formation of red blood cells and the development of metabolic reactions. Lack of iron may lead to anaemia, symptoms of which can include headaches, breathlessness and general lethargy. Foods high in iron include spinach, liver and chickpeas.

Sodium

Sodium is vital in balancing the fluids within the body and is present in meat, vegetables and salt.

FIND OUT

Go to http://www.eatwell.gov.uk/healthydiet/eatwellplate/ and find out what the Eatwell plate is and what proportion of each food group is shown on the Eatwell plate.

CHECK YOUR KNOWLEDGE

1 What is the difference between complex and simple carbohydrate?

2 Why is vitamin C essential to the body?

3 Give examples of both saturated and unsaturated fat.

Guidelines

The government has launched a variety of guidelines linked to initiatives for the health of the UK population. One is 'five a day', which encourages individuals to eat five named portions of fruit and vegetables a day. Another guideline is the government Eatwell plate (see Chapter 13.2). The idea behind this initiative is that by eating healthily, people reduce the risk of heart disease and cancer while maintaining a healthy weight. In addition to this, the body ingests the correct vitamins, minerals and antioxidants.

The Government 5 a Day logo

7.2 Customer needs

A chef has to be aware of the needs of the customers, not only with regard to items on the menu, but also to cater for special dietary needs, such as vegetarianism, diabetes or religious considerations such as halal.

Health

Customers have a wide variety of needs including allergies, modified diets and particular conditions.

Allergies

The NHS describes an allergy as an adverse reaction that the body has to a particular substance. Common allergies are those featuring shellfish, peanuts, wheat and dairy. When writing menus, a chef may not indicate every time milk or butter is used. However, it is common practice to highlight where nuts or nut products have been used (see list in Chapter 9.6 page 135).

Special conditions

The chef needs to be flexible and adapt to the needs of the customer. For example, customers may want low fat, low sugar (especially for diabetics), low sodium (salt) and high fibre. It is the job of the serving staff to communicate between the customer and the staff within the kitchen any special dietary needs.

Religion

It is up to the caterer to be aware of different religions affecting the preparation cooking and serving of food for example halal and kosher. Both types of food are promoted by the religion's dietary laws.

Halal

Islam prohibits certain items for the diets of believers, for example, pork, alcohol and foods made from animal fats. Islam involves individuals fasting during the sunlight hours of Ramadan.

Animals prepared following the guidelines have been slaughtered following the rules of Islam and this is called halal meat. The blood from the animals is drained away to prevent followers of Islam from consuming any blood or blood-related products.

Signs such as these warn customers of the presence of nuts in products

CASE STUDY

Joe Brown has a nut allergy. He visited the Olive Branch cafe and ate a piece of carrot cake which made him extremely ill. The waiter said there were no nuts in it but actually the recipe included walnuts.

- What should the café have done to prevent this?

CASE STUDY

Catherine Thompson is a coeliac which means she has a severe allergy to gluten. When she eats in a restaurant she has to avoid all wheat-based bread, pastry and pasta dishes and also cakes and biscuits. Catherine also has to check if gluten has been used in sauces and soups.

- As a chef, why is it important to have a good knowledge of allergies?

Kosher

Again this food meets the religious dietary laws, in this case, Jewish. Kosher food laws are rather complicated. For example:

- Fish and meat cannot be served together.
- Milk and meat cannot be served together.
- Any processed food must be prepared in the presence of the Rabbi.
- Kosher kitchens maintain different sets of utensils and equipment for different tasks and the equipment cannot be mixed.

Vegetarian

The three main types of vegetarians are lacto-ovo vegetarians, vegans and fruitarians.

- Lacto-ovo vegetarians also eat eggs and dairy produce in addition to vegetables and any derivatives such as fromage frais, cream and yoghurts.
- Vegans do not eat dairy produce and follow a strict regime of fruit, vegetables, pulses, grains and nuts. In some cases, vegans refuse to utilise any animal produce including leather for shoes and belts.
- Fruitarians only eat the fruit of a plant and do not eat any vegetables that have been 'killed' to provide for human consumption. Fruitarians can suffer from hyperglycaemia or diabetes due to the fact that fruit contains a high level of sugar.

Children

The needs of children have to be considered when ordering food for the menus. The children's menu should not just be seen as modifying the portion sizes that adults receive. It should be a way to both appeal to the needs of children while maintaining a balanced diet. All too often, children are restricted to unimaginative stereotypical food such as fish fingers and chips, and jelly and ice cream. With the right balance of flavours and presentation, children can be persuaded to eat a more nutritious meal while maintaining a balance of all the essential sources of vitamins and minerals.

Kosher food is a key part of Jewish culture

ACTIVITY

You are the chef in charge of a kosher banquet. What considerations should be given while preparing the food in the kitchen? You may use the Internet to further research this topic.

TRY THIS

Design and make a vegan main course to fulfil the recommended daily allowance of protein.

ACTIVITY

You have been given the responsibility of organising a function for a party of 20 vegetarians. What questions should you ask the party host and what information should you provide the kitchen with?

CHECK YOUR KNOWLEDGE

1 Give examples of different allergies that can effect an individual.
2 Give examples of special conditions where a chef needs to adapt to the needs of the customer.
3 Give examples of different types of vegetarian.

7.3 Types of menus

There are a whole host of menus available to the caterer depending on the type of establishment, the occasion and time of day, for example, lunch or dinner, café or à la carte, Valentine's day or Christmas, wedding or christening.

Table d'hôte

This term literally means in French 'the host's table' but in menu planning terms, means a 'fixed price' menu. For example, a customer might have a choice of three starters, three main courses and three desserts all for £15. Dishes on this menu tend to be made from lower-cost ingredients, for example, chicken breast as opposed to duck breast.

Cooking methods tend to focus on heartier methods of cookery, for example, braising a joint of beef as opposed to pan frying a fillet of beef.

TABLE D'HÔTE MENU
Two courses £18.50

STARTERS

Soupe a l'Oignon
With a Cheese Crouton

Shetland Smoked Salmon & Crayfish Salad
With a Lime & Basil Dressing

Grilled Goats Cheese
With Leaves, Croutons, Olive Oil, Garlic & Basil

Chicken Liver Terrine
Wrapped in Bacon With a Red Onion Jam

MAIN COURSES

Aberdeen Angus 8oz Rump Steak in a Mushroom sauce
Served with Fries and mixed vegetables

Tartiflette
Potato, Onion & Leek Fondant Topped With Reblochon Cheese
Served with Mixed Leaf Salad with a Lime Herb Dressing

Grilled Fillet of Scottish Salmon in a Lemon sauce
Served with Basmati Rice

A table d'hôte menu

À la carte

À la carte refers to individually priced dishes placed on an extensive menu. Usually, if a customer eats à la carte, it is usually the case that the dishes contain more expensive ingredients, for example, roasted saddle of venison with a wild mushroom and port sauce.

For this menu, the customer has more freedom to make up their own menu, usually from a choice of more than six starters, main course and desserts. For the privilege of choosing from this menu, higher overall costs are charged.

FIRST COURSE

Chicken liver parfait with apple and cider chutney and warm brioche	£8.50
Smoked guinea fowl salad with caramelised fig chutney	£10.15
Pea and ham soup with pancetta crisp	£5.75
Salmon tartare with cucumber salad	£12.25
Goats cheese terrine with aubergine and red pepper	£8.65
Wild mushroom risotto with truffle oil	£7.50

SECOND COURSE

MEAT

Confit leg of duck with cassoulet beans and creamed potato	£18.75
Aged fillet of Aberdeen Angus beef with root vegetables, roast potatoes and béarnaise sauce	£26.75
Lemon and thyme roast breast of free range chicken, crushed sweet potato and swede with wild mushroom sauce	£19.15
Pan fried sea bass with potato, spinach, poached fennel and saffron dressing	£23.75
Grilled sea bream with king prawn colcannon and cockle broth	£19.75
Gorgonzola tart with roasted cherry vine tomatoes, soft herbs and balsamic dressing	£10.50
Ricotta, almond and spinach open lasagne and roasted red pepper vinaigrette	£12.50

PUDDINGS (all £6.75)

Apple and thyme tart tatin served with vanilla ice cream
Lemon posset with fruit compote
Vanilla panacotta and balsamic berries
Chocolate terrine

An à la carte menu

Themed

A big hotel or restaurant could offer a variety of themes depending on the occasion. Some examples of this could include a special meal for Burns Night, Halloween, Valentine's Day, and St Patrick's Day. Generally, the meal reflects the occasion so for Valentine's Day, the meal would consist of special dishes worded to sound romantic and could use symbolic ingredients including truffles, oysters and champagne.

For these occasions, the restaurant is decorated to suit the theme with specialist table cloths, centrepieces, balloons and uniforms for staff, for example, on St Patrick's Day.

Celebration

A celebration could be a variety of things but usually refers to birthdays, christenings, anniversaries, Christmas and New Year. Depending on religion, it can include Hanukkah, Ramadan, Eid, Passover and many more.

Valentine's Day is a popular restaurant theme

A large hotel frequently employs somebody in charge of liaising with customers for special occasions, for example, weddings. This person would give customers a whole range of choices relating to type of menu, colours within the room, flowers on the table, special gifts for guests, celebration cake through to musical arrangements for the special occasion.

Conference and function

Conferences can be held in a range of locations including restaurants, hotels, and specialist conference facilities. A conference centre is more suited to providing delegates with the business facilities including seating, multimedia and general administrative services. In addition to this, the clients would receive catering facilities from hot beverages through to a three-course meal.

Functions can either be for business or private clients and can involve either a fixed price sit-down meal or buffet. An example of a function is a local business bringing their employees in for a meal with 100 covers and a £15 spend.

TRY THIS

Plan a range of materials for St Patrick's Day:

1 Plan the menu (one starter, one main course and one dessert).
2 Develop a table plan (100 customers).
3 List the themed materials for room decoration.

CHECK YOUR KNOWLEDGE

1 What is à la carte?
2 What themes are available to the caterer in a large hotel?
3 What choices are available for a person planning a wedding?

7.4 Fast food

Fast food and takeaways

There could be an argument that anything prepared in a short amount of time could be classed as 'fast food', for example, a sandwich or a pizza. To most people fast food means burgers, fish and chips and kebabs. But it also includes Chinese and Indian takeaways as well as sandwich shops.

Most fast food outlets need specialist equipment that restricts menu planning.

Fish and chip shops

A fixed menu is available to customers, and lists all of the available products including the traditional battered cod with mushy peas and chips. Here is an example of the dishes available from a chip shop:

Fish
Regular Cod – £3.65
Large Cod – £4.75
Haddock – £3.95
Plaice – £3.95
Lemon Sole – £4.15
Rock – £3.75
Hake – £3.45

Chips
Regular – £1.30
Large – £1.90

Pies
Steak and Kidney – £1.90
Beef and Onion – £1.90
Chicken and Mushroom – £1.90

Chicken (Finest Suffolk Chicken)
Burgers
Beef Burger (1/4 Pounder) – £1.90
Cheese Burger (1/4 Pounder) – £2.00
Special Cheese Burger (1/2 Pounder) – £2.95
Veggie Burger – £1.80
Veggie Burger (with Cheese) – £1.90
Chicken Burger – £2.85
Chicken Burger (With Cheese) – £2.95

Sausages
Sausage (Regular) – 75p
Sausage (Large) – £1.30
Battered Sausage (Regular) – 85p
Battered Sausage (Jumbo) – £1.40

Children's Menu
Cod and Chips – £2.85
Sausage and Chips – £1.35
Fish Cake and Chips – £1.35
Fish Fingers and Chips – £2.35
Chicken Nuggets (3) and Chips – £2.60
Kids Soft Drink – 25p

Extras
Mushy Peas (Regular) – 60p
Mushy Peas (Large) – 90p
Baked Beans (Regular) – 60p
Baked Beans (Large) – 90p
Curry Sauce (Regular) – 60p
Curry Sauce (Large) – 90p
Gravy (Regular) – 60p
Gravy (Large) – 90p
Bread Roll – 40p
Chip Buttie – £1.20

Drinks
Cans – 65p
Water (500 ml) – 65p

A standard chip shop menu

In menu planning terms, the dishes that are served relate to a base of general ingredients and can be varied depending on customer requirements. For example, the chips, gravy and mushy peas can be served with any of the main products.

The caterer needs to consider what equipment is available when planning the menu. The main cooking method is deep frying and so changes to the menu would have to take into account how the new ingredients would be cooked and whether it is economical to invest in new equipment.

Indian takeaway

When planning a menu for an Indian takeaway, you need to consider the size of the establishment, the huge range of available dishes, the fact that some of the ingredients need marinating and the extensive choice of herbs and spices. One advantage is that a lot of dishes can be made by varying the same ingredients, which in menu planning terms, gives the customer a huge amount of variety.

Equipment is a huge consideration when standard ovens, hobs and grills are required in addition to more specialist equipment, including a tandoor which is a cylindrical clay oven used for roasting and baking. Examples of dishes produced in a tandoor are chicken tikka and naan bread.

Chinese takeaway

Chinese takeaways feature very fast wok cookery using fresh vegetables, meats, fish and specialist ingredients, such as water chestnuts, bamboo shoots and bean sprouts. Similar to Indian cookery, a whole variety of dishes can be made from the same ingredients. When planning a menu for Chinese cookery, a range of cooking methods are used, including stir-frying, deep frying and steaming. Extensive pre-prepared ingredients are available to complement the flavours within the dishes, including hoi sin, soy sauce, black bean and nampla.

Burger restaurants

The popular burger restaurants operate a franchise system. This means that the owners need to use the corporate logo, standard menus and prices, follow standard procedures and buy ingredients from designated suppliers. In real terms, customers recognise particular burgers and meal deals. In menu planning for a franchise system, all the materials are already provided and it is up to the caterer just to follow the standard procedures to produce the food.

Smaller burger takeaways exist using similar formats, for example, meal deals, a range of burgers and accompaniments, but are allowed total freedom with menu planning. Some businesses use a chalk board to show offers and promotions.

A tandoor oven is used in many Indian restaurants

ACTIVITIES

1 Invent a new Chinese main course dish suitable to be packaged and taken away by a customer.
2 Name two advantages and two disadvantages of producing food within a fish and chip shop.

CHECK YOUR KNOWLEDGE

1 Why does the caterer need to consider available equipment when planning a menu?
2 Which culture features a tandoor oven?
3 What is a franchise system?

7.5 Types of dishes

This section goes through the whole menu, starting with soups and starters, through to hot and cold desserts. In addition to this, accompaniments and snacks are also featured. It is important that the caterer is aware of different commodities available for each course and how courses complement each other.

Starters

Soups

The right soup is needed for the right occasion or meal. For example, a broth or a chunky soup is more appropriate for lunch, whereas a cream soup or consommé is more suitable for dinner.

The requirements of the customer also need to be considered. For example, for a function serving rugby players, a hearty oxtail soup might be more fitting than cream of broccoli soup.

Cold starters

A range of cold starters could be made available to customers including those needing limited preparation, for example, Scottish smoked salmon and cured continental meats.

Other items needing more preparation include a variety of salads, patés, terrines and brushettas. The key with menu planning is variety and extensive use of imagination.

Hot starters

Depending on the style of restaurant, whether the meal is lunch or dinner and whether the menu is à la carte or table d'hôte, dishes could include a sea-fish brochette marinated in lemon grass and fresh thyme or pan-fried chicken livers with pink peppercorns and a herb brioche.

A terrine

As a rule of thumb, as long as different ingredients are featured and the dishes produced can be prepared in a reasonably short period of time, then a whole range of choice is available to the caterer.

Main courses

The caterer needs to consider different cooking methods when planning main courses. Using à la carte as an example, then duck confit is poached, a lamb shank is braised and a beef fillet could be pan-fried or grilled. It is also important to take into account the available equipment and the skills of the staff when developing the main course section of an à la carte menu.

Sauces are used to complement the flavours of the different dishes. For example, a delicate cream sauce could complement the light texture of a fish dish.

Accompaniments

Tradition plays a large part with a number of accompaniments. For example, roast beef is accompanied by Yorkshire puddings, horseradish sauce and onion gravy. Customers expect turkey at Christmas to arrive with bread sauce, cranberry sauce, chestnut stuffing and pigs-in-blankets (sausages rolled in bacon).

The rules can be adapted. For example, roasted beef fillet could be served with a horseradish crust and fondant potatoes instead of roast potatoes.

Desserts

Cold desserts

When planning a dessert menu, a general rule could be to feature something fruity, something chocolate and something with pastry. Sample dishes could include a variety of tarts, for example, chocolate, lemon and fruits of the forest. Other dishes include rice puddings, fruit mousses, gateaux and meringues.

A special dessert served in a restaurant

Plated desserts allow the caterer more freedom to decorate the dishes with either coulis or sauces with complementary garnishes.

Hot desserts

Sometimes customers enjoy the option of a hot dessert and this can be in the form of something quite delicate or hearty, for example, a traditional jam roly poly with custard or a rich sticky toffee pudding with a butterscotch sauce.

Snacks

These are usually centred around a bread or pastry base. Examples of these are: grilled chicken Panini, goat's cheese and sun-blushed tomato focaccia, a Chinese dim sum and a red onion and broccoli quiche.

Snacks take many forms and often take influences from a variety of different cultures.

TRY THIS

1 Develop a dessert menu for serving in a golf club.
2 Create a simple snack for serving in a vegetarian café.
3 Adapt a traditional Christmas dinner in an individual way.

CHECK YOUR KNOWLEDGE

1 Name three hot starters that could be served in a restaurant or hotel.
2 What are accompaniments?
3 Suggest examples of available snacks for a gym.

7.6 Menu planning 1 (Contrast)

A successful menu should provide customers with a variety of contrasting dishes. The caterer can control and vary many aspects of the menu, such as cultural influences, ingredients, cooking methods, flavour, texture and colour in order to provide a varied and interesting menu, which is also profitable.

Cultural influences

Some restaurants are based around a particular culture or theme, for example, gourmet, Italian or Thai. It is expected that an Italian restaurant will serve Italian food like pizza and pasta. However, in an establishment without a specialist theme, it is possible to mix cultural influences when menu planning.

Today's chefs have the choice to mix and match from a variety of cultures, countries and continents to provide the consumer with more choice than ever before. With the internet, it is becoming easier to investigate different cultures, explore the different dishes and to adapt those dishes to the needs of the customer.

An Italian restaurant enjoying great success by serving classic Italian food

Commodities (ingredients) and seasons

Cost

As a general rule, the cost of ingredients within a dish must be balanced. For example, the use of an expensive ingredient like asparagus could be offset against a cheaper ingredient like rice to make the perfect risotto. The end result is happy customers and an affordable dish.

Match to establishment menu plan

The ingredients must match the menu being served. For example, in a particular establishment, using beef fillet on a 'menu of the day' at lunch may be using an ingredient that is normally reserved for an à la carte menu in the evening.

Seasonal ingredients

The caterer has the opportunity to develop creative and innovative menus by using seasonal ingredients such as pumpkin, which is available around the end of October. This means that the food does not have to be imported from another country and therefore is fresh and at the best possible price. Using food obviously out of season can give a negative impression for example, where a chef may put grouse on the menu during July. Since the grouse shooting season starts on 12 August, customers may quite reasonably think that the dish may have come from the freezer and is not freshly made.

Cooking methods and nutrition

Different customers have different needs and desires when looking at a menu. A good menu will have dishes made using a variety of cooking methods, so an à la carte menu could feature pan-fried duck, poached fillet of bream and roasted root vegetables. This variety allows customers to choose something that suits their needs.

For many customers, if they see too much deep-fried food on a menu, they get the impression that the establishment may be downmarket. A well-chosen menu gives customers the choice of either something healthy, for example, poached fish or something less healthy such, as deep-fried cod in a beer batter.

Flavour, texture and colour

Important aspects to consider when planning a menu are flavour, texture and colour.

Flavour

By contrasting the flavours within a menu, dishes appear more appealing to clients. For example, a menu full of dishes using cream sauces will not appeal to someone who would prefer a tomato-based sauce or something spicier.

Colours can be as important as flavour and texture

Textures

Textures are important in order to provide customers with a satisfying eating experience. One person might prefer a poached brill dish with a delicate texture while another person might order a rare steak, which provides a more succulent and firm texture. Textures can also be varied on the same plate, for example, by serving a beef fillet with smooth mashed potato and crunchy (al dente) carrots.

Colours

Generally customers prefer food that looks appealing. Giving colour to a dish makes the ingredients appear more vibrant and exciting. By contrasting the rich green colour of asparagus against the bright red of vine tomatoes, a chef can enhance the more subtle colouring of the chicken breast and give the meal more visual appeal.

THE IVY RESTAURANT SETTLE

Function Menu
13TH OCTOBER 2005

CREAM OF CAULIFLOWER SOUP
Cauliflour soup served with crisp bacon and a mini baguette

GUINEU FOWL CASSEROLE
Guinea fowl infused with ginger, thyme and majoram finished in cream sauce

CREAM BRULE
Accompanied by a crème anglaise or a lump of homemade ice-cream

Coffeee at the waiters digression!

£35.00

THE IVY RESTRANT SETTLE

Lunch Menu
13TH OCTOBER 2005

LEEK & POTATO SOUP
Lavishly gathered tender garden leeks delicately boiled with cubes of Maris Piper potatoes finished with our homemade chicken stock

FILLET OF SCOTTISH BEEF
Tender beef fillet pan-fried in dripping with a wild mushroom cream sauce, chipped potatoes, fois gras and bacon lardons

CHOIX DE DESSERT
With warm custard

ACTIVITY

1 Look at the menus above and list the faults.

2 Give suggestions on how to improve the menu.

3 Suggest common faults in menu planning.

CHECK YOUR KNOWLEDGE

1 What are the benefits of using food in season?

2 How can the chef incorporate cultural influences into the menu?

3 Which cookery methods are considered healthy?

7.7 Menu planning 2 (Business needs)

Portion control

When planning a menu, it is vital that the caterer considers portion control, for example, if a salmon dish is on an à la carte menu then a main course portion could be approximately 200 grams. In real terms, this means:

- The customer has a consistent amount.
- The caterer knows what each customer is receiving.
- The dish can be reliably costed.
- Complaints regarding portion size should not be an issue.
- Standard size can also equal standard cooking time.

When cooking for a family, portion control might not seem as important. However, when catering on a mass scale, the impact on profit can be large. There are a number of ways available to the caterer to reliably portion ingredients, including using:

- scales to weigh ingredients, for example beef fillet
- measuring jugs, for example, for sauces for a large buffet
- soup ladle, for example consistent amounts for a lunchtime service
- trays, for example 12 portions of bread and butter pudding from each tray
- food rings, for example, cheesecakes for a large function
- ramekin dishes, for example, individual crème brulée for a gourmet restaurant.

CASE STUDY

Geoff is the head chef at the local golf club. During the week he has many functions serving hundreds of customers. Geoff is in trouble because even though his food is excellent, his food costs are too high. It has been pointed out that his portion sizes vary. For example, one customer was served a steak that filled the plate while on the next table a customer got one that only filled half the plate.

- What are the consequences to Geoff and the business if he continues with different portion sizes?
- How can Geoff ensure correct portion control?

There are several different types of measuring tools

Cost of raw materials

The cost of raw materials needs to be taken into account when planning a menu. For example, using asparagus out of season means that produce from abroad needs to be sourced and the cost of the dish could increase.

By being aware of the cost of available produce, the caterer can take advantage of both seasonal and daily offers by a variety of suppliers. For example, a fish supplier might offer black bream at a special price. This would mean that the caterer could put a speciality dish on the specials board and customers would get the variety they deserve.

Constraints

Skills of chef

As a caterer, you have developed an à la carte menu with seven different starters, main courses and desserts, each with various complex methods, but you have forgotten to consider the skills of the chef. Consider the impact that this might have on the smooth operating of the business if the chef isn't up to scratch. Here are some points listed below:

- inconsistent preparation and cooking of the dishes
- inconsistent portion control resulting in loss of profit
- complaints by customers
- loss of reputation
- closure of business.

Types of outlet

When developing a menu, you need to consider the type of outlet. For example, a bread and butter pudding could be served everywhere from a roadside café to a Michelin-starred restaurant. The presentation in the roadside café would be far simpler and the ingredients might not be as rich. The Michelin-starred restaurant would use superior butter, double cream, possibly brioche instead of bread, and the time taken to create the dish would be far longer.

Time

Customers expect to receive their meals within a certain time frame so, when ordering a burger, individuals expect their food within a matter of minutes. However, when ordering a well-done steak, it is accepted that the waiting time will be extended.

In a café, the food needs to be available in a fairly short time span because most customers want to dine in a short period of time.

ACTIVITY

Use a shopping website to compare the cost of 1 kg each of potatoes, cheese and chicken and a tin of beans. Put the commodities in order of cost and discuss the importance of the cost of ingredients when deciding on portion size.

TRY THIS

Work in pairs to produce two different bread and butter puddings, one to serve in a cafe for 99p and one that includes an accompaniment to serve in a fine dining restaurant for £4.95.

CHECK YOUR KNOWLEDGE

1 What is the advantage for the caterer of rigid portion control?
2 List eight different ways to portion ingredients.
3 Find out the cost of one item, for example, beef fillet from three different sources and compare costs and quality. You may use the internet.

ExamCafé

Exam preparation

Revision checklist

Which exam	Content	What to revise
All for catering	Nutrition and healthy eating	You need to know the difference between simple and complex carbohydrates. You should be aware of both the saturated and unsaturated fats. You should understand the function of protein in the body. You need to have an awareness of different vitamins and minerals.
All for catering	Customer needs	You need to know customer needs relating to special conditions. You should be aware of any special considerations including religions or beliefs. You should understand the menu planning needs of children.
All for catering	Types of menu	You should know the different between Table d'hôte and à la carte. You should have an awareness of different occasions and celebrations that might require a special menu. You should understand how a caterer can develop function and conference menus.
All for catering	Fast food	You should be aware of different types of fast food menus. You should know suitable dishes for a fast food menu.
All for catering	Types of dishes	You need to know the different courses and accompaniments within a menu. You should know a range of dishes for each course.
All for catering	Menu planning 1 (Contrast)	You should be aware of a range of contrasting factors to be considered when planning a menu. You should have some awareness of seasonal produce. You should understand the importance of flavour, texture and colour.
All for catering	Menu planning 2 (Business needs)	You should understand the various methods of portion control available to the caterer. You need to be aware of the costs of raw ingredients. You need to understand the constraints of a business relating to menu planning.

Activities

This is a knowledge based unit of work that needs learning. The needs of the customer, awareness of facilities, types of menus and dishes all need remembering.

Exam preparation

Use past exam questions to check your knowledge. Most of the questions are about your knowledge and will ask you to apply your understanding to selected questions. Some questions might relate to catering terminology.

Sample question

A local catering company is offering to plan, prepare and cook for children's parties. Plan a suitable menu including two savoury dishes, one sweet dish and a drink. (5 marks)

Examiner's tip
Remember this party is for children so try to avoid spicy food, alcohol and any food which children might see as being too complex.

Sample answer

Savoury:
- Pasta
- Jacket potatoes
- Sausages
- Mild curry and rice
- Pizza
- Pastry
- Burgers or other fast food option
- Variety of sandwiches

Sweet:
- Ice cream
- Jelly
- Gateaux
- A range of different cakes and sponges
- Biscuits
- Tarts, for example lemon or jam

Drink:
- Fruit juices
- Smoothies
- Fizzy drinks
- Milkshakes or milk

Sample question

What should the catering company consider when planning the children's party? (6 marks)

Examiner's tip
Think about the party both from the kitchen point of view and from the restaurant serving point of view.

Sample answer

The following should be considered when planning a children's party:

- Special requirements – for example, vegetarians, coeliacs or someone with a low fat diet.
- Allergies – it is important to know if someone has a nut allergy to avoid any potential harm to an individual.
- Season – seasonal goods can provide customers with more variety and fresh ingredients whilst providing the business with a most cost effective purchase of supplies.
- Kitchen facilities – if the kitchen only has one fat fryer, and half the food is deep fat fried, then the kitchen may run into trouble.
- Age of the children – some children may be older and want more adult food.
- Where the food will be served – if the food is served in a marquee then there are adequate storage and cooling facilities.
- Food costs – bulk buying could help reduce the overall cost.

Chapter 8

FOOD PREPARATION AND COOKING

8.1 Meat and poultry

This section is broken down into two main areas: firstly food groups, a variety of commodities including meat, fish and vegetables, which focuses on selection, storage and preparation. Secondly, methods of cookery are explored, highlighting technical language with explanation and selected recipes.

Meat is generally thought of as products bought from a butcher, such as beef, lamb, and pork. Poultry is classed as any domestically reared bird for example: chicken, turkey, duck (not wild) and guinea fowl.

Quality points when purchasing

All meat and poultry should be sourced locally where possible, as this should ensure that the food is fresher and more reasonably priced because it doesn't include additional handling and transportation costs. Organic quite often equals a tastier meat or poultry.

Poultry

Consider the following when buying poultry:
- Packaging: is the packaging damaged and is there a use by date?
- Condition of the flesh: are there any broken bones or blood spots (if so the poultry is not in prime condition).
- Smell: it should smell fresh and there should be no unpleasant odour.
- There should be no stickiness.

Beef

There are many different cuts to choose from when buying beef, but here are a few guidelines:
- Buy beef from a good butcher.
- The beef should be a brown-red, not the bright red that you sometimes see in supermarkets.
- Depending on the cut, there should be marbling on the beef (fat specks).
- There should be no stickiness or unpleasant odour.

Lamb

Lamb has less cuts to choose from than beef but there are still a number of points to consider including:
- Buy lamb from a reputable supplier.
- The lamb should be a deep brown.
- The fat should be a cream colour.
- There should be no stickiness or unpleasant odour.

Pork

When buying pork from a butcher, consider the following:
- No stickiness or unpleasant odours should be present.
- No green tinge on the flesh.
- No blood spots or broken bones should be visible.

When selecting beef, lamb or pork, note than some of the cuts are better for roasting, some better for braising and some better for pan frying. This will be covered in more detail in the cooking sections in Chapters 8.6 – 8.9.

Storage

In a catering store in a large hotel, there will be a walk-in fridge, which allows separate sections for meat and poultry to be stored. The poultry should be stored well away from beef and lamb. All the meat and poultry should be stored at a temperature of between 3–5˚C. Under no circumstances should poultry blood be allowed to drip over any other product due to risk of cross-contamination.

Preparation

All meats should be prepared separately using a red chopping board, or other chopping board specially set aside for the task. Any preparations done should be kept separately to again minimise risk of cross-contamination.

Boning

This involves the removal of selected bones in certain joints of meat. For example, the bones can be removed from a leg of lamb to make the carving and portion control far easier. This is also the case when removing the bones from a shoulder of pork for a casserole or stew. To complete this task effectively, a sharp boning knife should be used.

Tying

You can secure a joint for roasting with string, using a series of loops. This allows the meat to stay in one place and keeps the stuffing within the joint.

Stuffing

You can make stuffing for either meat or poultry. It both enhances the flavour and texture. Once the stuffing has been made, you need to cool it before placing in a cavity within the joint or poultry.

Batting

You can use a meat hammer to flatten either a small piece of meat or poultry. This has the effect of breaking down the connective tissue and tenderises the meat.

Marinading

Aromatic herbs, spices, vegetables, wine and vinegar can all create a liquor, which over time both tenderises and gives flavour to selected cuts of meat. An example of this is a lime, coriander and garlic marinade which you can use to tenderise chicken.

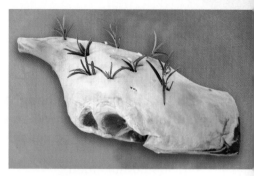

Herbs over time can both tenderise and give extra flavour to meat

ACTIVITY

Complete the table below to show different preparation methods relating to a range of cuts of meat and poultry.

Preparation method	Cut of meat or poultry
	chicken leg
boning	
	fillet of beef
tying	
	shoulder of Lamb
	duck breast
marinating	

CHECK YOUR KNOWLEDGE

1 State the quality point of buying a leg of lamb.
2 What is a marinade?
3 When should a joint of meat be secured by tying?

8.2 Fish

Quality points

Fish should always be bought as fresh as possible from a reputable fishmonger. When selecting fish, the following information should be considered:

- It should not smell unpleasant.
- Fish should have a good amount of slime.
- Round fish generally should have plenty of scales and red gills.
- Eyes should be bright and not sunken.
- Flesh should be firm.

Storage

Fish should be stored in a walk-in fridge or a separate area away from other products at a temperature of 0–5˚C. Some establishments pack fish in ice to keep it fresh.

A fishmonger will sell a number of different types of fish

Types of fish

Fish can be categorised in two ways: white, oily and shellfish or round, flat and oily fish. The preparation and cooking of one fish is similar to that of another fish in the same category. For example, the same preparation method used to fillet a plaice can be applied when filleting a halibut, the only difference being that the halibut is much bigger.

Round	Flat	Oily
coley	halibut	anchovies
cod	turbot	sardines
haddock	brill	tuna
sea bass	skate	mackerel
black bream	plaice	herring
grey mullet	sole	salmon

Preparation of a whole round fish

- First, scale the fish by using either a scaling device or the back of a boning knife.
- Then remove the fins.
- Gut the fish and remove the intestines.
- Wash the insides and dry using a clean cloth.
- Fillet the fish using a filleting knife. Remove both fillets from either side of the backbone.
- Trim away any bones and, using a pair of tweezers, remove the pin bones (the little bones running down the length of the fillet).
- Skin the fish.

Cuts of fish

The following shows different cuts of fish using both round and flat categories.

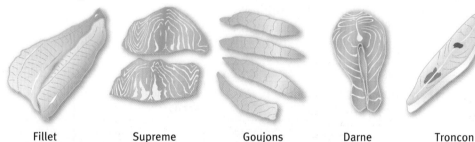

| Fillet | Supreme | Goujons | Darne | Troncon | Paupiette |

Some of the common fish cuts

Coating fish

Pane

An example of pane is when goujons or strips of fish are passed through seasoned flour, egg wash and breadcrumbs. Note that pane should be done in three separate trays to ensure proper coverage of the fish. The pane protects the fish in the fryer and gives a crispy coating.

Batter

Using flour, eggs and milk, you can make a batter, for example, for a fillet of haddock. The ingredients can be varied, for example, beer can be used instead of the milk and cornflour can be added to alter the texture.

Marinading fish

You can make marinade in a similar way to those in the meat section, however fish marinades tend to use more fresh herbs and citrus flavourings. Fish generally requires less time to get a good result, with some marinades needing less than 15 minutes.

ACTIVITY

Find a recipe that uses each of the cuts of fish below.

CHECK YOUR KNOWLEDGE

1 What is a pane?
2 Name four flat fish and suggest a fish preparation.
3 List the quality points of a whole salmon.

8.3 Fruit and vegetables

Vegetables

When purchasing vegetables, you should consider:

- Is the packaging damaged and within the sell-by date?
- Are any of the vegetables bruised or damaged?
- Are the vegetables firm to touch (depending on the vegetable)?
- Organic vegetables often contain more flavour, less pesticides and support local producers.

Vegetables should be stored in a cool, dark environment, in a fridge or larder. You need to make sure that no pests or rodents are encouraged by improper storage of ingredients.

Vegetables are classified in such a way that once a basic principle of cookery has been learned, it can be applied to other vegetables within the same family. For example, potatoes can be cooked in the same way as sweet potatoes or Jerusalem artichokes.

Roots	Tubers	Bulbs	Flowerheads	Stems and shoots	Leafy	Pods and seeds	Fruiting	Fungi
carrots	potatoes	onion	broccoli	celery	cabbage	peas	squash	mushrooms
parsnips	yam	garlic	cauliflower	beansprouts	spinach	mangetout	pumpkin	truffles
turnips	sweet potatoes	shallot	globe artichoke	kohlrabi	Swiss chard	butter beans	marrow	cepes

Once vegetables have been washed, peeled or seeded (depending on the vegetables) they can be prepared into a variety of specialist vegetable cuts.

Baton

Julienne

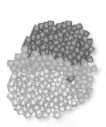
Brunoise

Macedoine

Mirepoix

Some of the common vegetable cuts

Fruit

When purchasing fruit, you should consider:

- Is the packaging damaged and within the sell-by date?
- Is any of the fruit bruised or damaged?
- Is the fruit firm to touch (depending on the fruit)?
- Organic fruit often contains more flavour, less pesticides and buying it supports local producers.

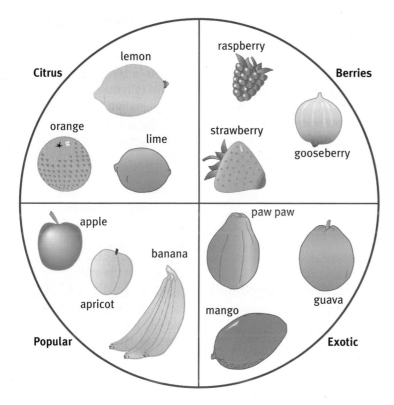

One way to categorise fruit

Fruit at home is stored in a fruit bowl. However, in a hotel, to stop deterioration it is stored in a refrigerator. Note that some fruit, for example, bananas, should be kept at room temperature and any fruit with a short shelf-life should be kept separately from fruit with a longer shelf-life.

Decorative preparations

Fanning

Fruits such as strawberries or melon can be cut using a knife to create a fanned effect.

Van Dyke

Using a knife or a specialist tool, a V shape is cut around the circumference of melon, for example, to create a toothed effect.

ACTIVITY

A fruit salad can be quite boring. As a chef, find five different types of exotic fruit to enhance the salad and use an alternative style of presentation to impress the customer.

FIND OUT

What is a mirepoix of vegetables?

CHECK YOUR KNOWLEDGE

1 Name three fruits suitable for a crumble.
2 What should you consider when purchasing fruit?
3 Give two examples of tuber vegetables.
4 Why should vegetables be stored in a cool, dark environment?

8.4 Dairy and eggs

Dairy produce

According to the Food Standards Agency's 'Eatwell plate' milk and dairy products are classified as milk, cheese, yoghurt and fromage frais. In this section, we have also included butter and cream, which are traditionally regarded as dairy produce.

Storage

Dairy produce should ideally be kept in the fridge away from any strong-smelling odours, such as fish or chopped onions. Cheese should be kept in its original wrapping, for example, the wax paper maintains a circulation of air around the cheese and allows it to breathe. Blue cheese should be thoroughly wrapped to avoid smells passing onto other food.

Milk

There are a number of different types of milk, including goat, buffalo, sheep and soy milk, but the most popular is cow's milk.

The three main types of cow's milk are whole- or full-fat milk, containing approximately 3.5 per cent fat, semi-skimmed milk, containing 1.7 per cent fat and skimmed milk containing 0.2 per cent fat.

Other processes relating to milk are condensed, sterilised, UHT (Ultra Heat Treated), homogenised, dried and flavoured.

Cream

Different types of creams include single, double, whipped, sour, clotted and synthetic. Single cream contains 18 per cent fat and is more suitable for pouring over desserts and incorporating into dishes. Double cream provides a richer taste and contains 48 per cent fat.

Whipping cream is more versatile and is suitable for a variety of desserts, sauces and other products. It contains 38 per cent fat. An alternative to whipping cream is crème fraîche with a fat content of 39 per cent. It can be used to complement desserts and be incorporated into dishes. Crème fraîche is really cream that has been treated with a bacterial culture. Low-fat versions are available for a more healthy option.

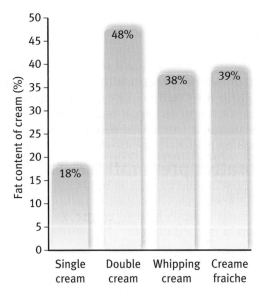

Fat content of cream

Butter

Butter is produced by churning fermented milk or cream. It is available in its purest form in either salted or unsalted versions. Alternatives to butter include margarine and a whole host of low-fat spreads. Butter can also be churned with olive oil to create an easier spreading fat.

Cheese

There are literally hundreds of cheeses to choose from, which provide the caterer with a huge amount of choice. The three main categories are hard, semi-hard and soft.

Hard cheeses	Semi-hard cheeses	Soft cheeses
parmesan	Lancashire	brie
emmenthal	Wensleydale	camembert
cheddar	edam	pont l'evêque
double gloucester	mozzarella	reblochon
	stilton	stinking bishop

Cheese is made by taking milk and adding an acidified bacterial culture with the addition of rennet to create curds (solids) and whey (liquid). The whey is drained and the curds remain and are processed to create cheese.

Eggs

Eggs are classified as a protein food in the Eatwell plate. The four main types of eggs are:
- Battery hens
- Barn hens
- Free-range hens
- Organic hens

These relate to the conditions in which the hens have been allowed to lay their eggs. **Battery hens** have confined conditions that restrict movement and consequently affect their natural behaviour. **Barn hens** have more space and are allowed to display natural behaviours such as flapping, roosting, nesting and stretching. **Free-range hens** have the freedom to roam around the farm but can be fed on genetically modified feed. **Organic hens** have both the freedom of movement that free-range hens have, but are fed an organic feed.

When purchasing eggs, it is important to consider the following points:
- Buy from a reputable supplier.
- Discard dirty or cracked eggs.
- Buy eggs with the Lion Mark (this is a sign that the eggs have been quality-checked).
- Eggs should have a best-before date stamped onto the shell.

A selection of some of the cheeses available on the market

ACTIVITY

Eggs are used to enrich food products but they are also used for other purposes. Give three other uses of eggs within cookery.

Give two alternatives to butter within cookery and state their uses.

CHECK YOUR KNOWLEDGE

1 State five examples of types of milk available to the caterer.
2 What should you consider when buying eggs?
3 Why do chefs use different types of cream?

8.5 Convenience and dry goods

Dry goods and convenience products in a large establishment such as a hotel, can either be stored in a larder or specialist stores. A specialist store could be managed by a stores technician or stores keeper who issues goods directly to areas within the hotel, such as the kitchen or the restaurant. Dry goods can be broken down into a variety of types. The following represents a section of these.

Flour

Flour is used in a multitude of pastry, bread, sponge, cake and savoury products. Generally, when making cakes you would use a **soft flour**, when making bread you would use **strong flour**. However, there are always exceptions to the rules. Different types of flours include:

- plain flour (soft)
- self-raising flour
- wholemeal flour
- rice flour
- spelt flour
- granary flour
- strong flour (strong)
- buckwheat flour
- gluten-free flour.

Flours can also be used as a thickening agent to stabilise sauces or sweet products. Here are three examples:

- arrowroot flour made from the root of the arrowroot plant
- cornflour made from ground maize
- potato flour also known as fecula.

Pasta

Pasta is made from either flour or semolina with the addition of egg, olive oil and a variety of flavourings, including spinach, sun-dried tomato, saffron and even squid ink (to give a black colour). Pasta can either be made with a pasta machine (bought commercially or domestically) or bought ready-made from a supplier. There are literally hundreds of different types of pasta and here are just a few:

- lasagna – sheets
- ravioli – envelopes of filled pasta
- tagliatelle – long thin strips of pasta
- cannelloni – tubes filled with a savoury mixture
- tortellini – pockets of filled pasta in the shape of a belly button
- vermicelli – meaning little worms.

Rice

Rice is generally broken down into long, medium and short grain.

One example of long-grain rice is Patna rice, which is used in a huge variety of dishes. Another type of long-grain rice is basmati with its aromatic and non-glutinous properties, which makes it dry and light and it does not separate when cooking.

An example of medium-grain rice is Arborio rice, which is primarily used in risotto. Another medium-grain rice is sushi rice which is used in Japanese cookery to create eye-catching and tasty appetisers.

An example of short-grain rice is Carolina rice, or rice pudding rice, which is used by chefs to create cold and hot rice pudding dishes.

Cereals and pulses

Alternatives to rice

- Cous cous are granules made from semolina.
- Bulgar wheat is a variety of middle-eastern manufactured wheat.
- Polenta is a golden-yellow Italian cornmeal. It can be ground coarsely or finely and is made from maize.
- Noodles – there is a huge variety of these – they are made from different flours, sometimes with the addition of egg.

Cereals and pulses

Cereals include buckwheat, pearl barley and oats. Pulses used within cookery could include split peas for pea soup, puy lentils to accompany a lamb dish, or chickpeas used to make hummus.

Oils

ACTIVITY

There are a whole range of convenience sauces and marinades on the market. List ten from a range of different cultures.

Oils

There are many different types of oils, from basic sunflower oil to olive oil costing hundreds of pounds. The type of oil to use depends on the dish or method of cookery, for example, olive oil could be used for frying a fillet of sea bass, sesame oil could be used to give flavour to noodles. Here are some examples of different oils:

- pumpkin seed oil
- walnut oil
- grapeseed oil
- groundnut oil
- flavoured oils, e.g. chilli, basil
- vegetable oil (generic term for a blend of oils).

Vinegars

You can use vinegars in cookery to enhance the flavours of dressings, marinades and a whole host of multi-cultural dishes. Popular examples include:

- balsamic vinegar
- malt vinegar
- rice vinegar
- white and red wine vinegar
- distilled vinegar
- flavoured vinegars including tarragon and thyme.

CHECK YOUR KNOWLEDGE

1 Name three different types of flour. What could you use each of them for?
2 Which types of rice is primarily used for risotto?
3 Give three alternatives to rice.

8.6 Boiling, steaming and poaching

Boiling

Boiling is the state of bringing a liquid to 100˚C. This turns the fluid into a vapour, which reduces any volume in the pan. A variety of meats, fish, poultry and vegetables can be boiled.

Blanching

There are a number of different uses for blanching, such as, to par cook or to remove the skin from vegetables.

Par cooking

For a large hotel or banqueting facility, it is sensible to par cook particular vegetables, for example, 300 portions of broccoli and carrots could be cooked to precisely the right degree and cooled, drained and presented ready for a function later on that day.

Removing the skin

To remove the skin from tomatoes, remove the core from the base of the tomato, place a criss-cross on the top of the tomato (to aid removal of the skin) and then place the tomatoes into boiling water for approximately 10 seconds (depending on type and ripeness of tomato). Then place the tomato into very cold or iced water until cool. The skin can then be easily removed.

Steaming

The three main ways to steam are by using a perforated container (domestic steamer), a **pressure steamer** or **atmospheric steamer**. Steaming is a nutritious method of cooking and ensures that the vitamins and minerals are not lost through the process of cooking. Take care when steaming food as it is quite easy to injure yourself from red-hot steam escaping the pan.

Poaching

Poaching is a slow method of cookery used for vegetables, meat, poultry, fish or eggs. This can either be shallow or deep. The deep method can be used to poach a whole salmon in a salmon kettle (long oblong container) in a liquid called a court bouillon. The shallow method is used to cook smaller pieces of meat, poultry or fish and is enhanced by aromatic vegetables and herbs. You can make a sauce from the cooking liquor. The liquid can be varied depending on the item being cooked, for example, salmon can be cooked in a white wine/fish stock mixture, whereas smoked haddock can be cooked in milk.

Steamers can be made for private use as well as industrial use

KEY TERMS

Pressure steamer: thick-walled pan with air-tight lid in which food is rapidly cooked by steam under high pressure.

Atmospheric steamer: food is placed in a steam chamber through which steam flows, cooking the food.

Recipes

Boiled shank of ham – serves 4

Ingredients:

4 ham shanks	2 bay leaves
1 whole onion	6 peppercorns

Method:

1 First soak the ham shanks overnight in cold water and wash thoroughly.

2 Place into a large saucepan, cover in cold water.

3 Cut the onion into a mirepoix (rough cut) and place into pan.

4 Add the bay leaves and peppercorns.

5 Bring to the boil and remove any resulting scum.

6 Simmer for three hours on a low heat until the ham shank is tender.

7 Allow the shanks to cool in the liquor.

8 Remove the skin from the shank.

9 The shank is now ready to be either used as a main course as baked ham shank (see Chapter 8.9) or used in a broth (both the meat and stock).

Steamed roulade of chicken – serves 4

Ingredients:

4 breasts of chicken (no skin or bone)

4 slices of Parma ham

8 large spinach leaves (washed with stalks removed)

50 g of pine kernels

Method:

1 Trim the chicken breast to remove any skin or fat.

2 Flatten the chicken breasts between two freezer bags until approximately 5 mm thick. Lay each breast onto a large square of cling film.

3 Place the Parma ham over the chicken breast followed by spinach leaves and a line of pine kernels.

4 Roll the roulade, taking care to make sure that the cling film is on the outside of the chicken and not rolled within the roulade itself.

5 Lift the roulade onto an additional sheet of cling film, roll and tie the edges.

6 Place the roulades into a steamer and cook for approximately 20 minutes (dependant on steamer and whether domestic or commercial).

7 Serve with an appropriate sauce.

FIND OUT

Using the internet or books, find dishes that can be poached. Include two food categories.

CHECK YOUR KNOWLEDGE

1 What is blanching?

2 Name three ways of steaming vegetables.

3 Name two liquids used to poach fish.

4 Why is steaming a nutritious and healthy method of cookery?

8.7 Braising and stewing

Braising

Braising is a combination of moist and dry heat whereby a piece of meat is first sealed in hot fat and then cooked slowly in a sauce or stock for a long time until tender.

Stewing

Stewing is similar to braising, except the pieces of meat or poultry or any other item are quite small and the resulting liquor is served as part of the dish. Stewing can be done either on the top of the oven in a pan, or alternatively in a casserole dish in the main oven.

Both stewing and braising are a healthy and nutritious way to cook different cuts of meat and poultry. The resulting liquor is extremely tasty and is used either strained or unstrained to complement the final dish.

Recipes

Braised shank of lamb – serves 4

Ingredients:

25 ml olive oil	2 tbsp plain flour
4 lamb shanks	1 tsp tomato purée
2 red onions	half a bottle of red wine
4 sprigs of fresh rosemary	2 l brown stock (lamb or beef)

Method:

1 Seal the lamb on all sides in a deep saucepan until brown.
2 Place lamb onto a plate and move to one side.
3 Add a rough dice of the onion and sweat with the rosemary.
4 Add the flour to make a roux and cook for one minute.
5 Add the tomato purée and start to slowly incorporate all of the liquid.
6 Put the lamb shanks back in the pan.
7 Cover with a lid.
8 Cook for approximately three hours or until tender in an oven at about 180°C or gas mark 4.
9 The lamb shank should be tender, yet still retain its shape.
10 Carefully remove the lamb shank and keep warm.
11 Correct the sauce by reducing to the right consistency and strain if required.
12 Serve the lamb shank with an appropriate accompaniment.

KEY TERMS

Sweat: cook without browning. For example, cooking onions in butter under a pan lid until soft but not brown.

Roux: a mixture of fat and flour used to thicken a soup or sauce.

Reduce: boil a sauce or liquid to reduce the volume and concentrate the flavour.

Beef and stout casserole – serves 4

Ingredients:

25 ml olive oil

600 g stewing beef (free from bone, fat or gristle)

2 shallots

4 sprigs of fresh thyme

2 tbsp plain flour

1 tsp tomato purée

1 can of good quality stout

2 l brown stock (lamb or beef)

Method:

1 Seal the beef in a deep saucepan until brown.

2 Add the sliced shallot and sweat with the chopped thyme.

3 Add the flour to make a roux and cook for one minute.

4 Add the tomato purée and start to slowly incorporate all of the liquid.

5 Cover with a lid.

6 Cook for approximately three hours or until tender in an oven at about 180°C or gas mark 4.

7 The beef should be tender yet still retain its shape.

8 If the sauce or liquor is too thin, some of the liquid could be drained into a separate pan and boiled to reduce the volume and returned to the meat.

9 Serve the beef with an appropriate accompaniment.

ACTIVITY

Taking the braised lamb shank recipe, develop three accompaniments that could be used on a main course plate within a top-class local restaurant. Explain how you decided what to use.

CHECK YOUR KNOWLEDGE

1 Define the term 'to seal'.

2 What is braising?

3 Give two types of meat suitable for stewing.

8.8 Frying (deep and shallow)

Deep frying

Using a temperature-controlled deep-fryer (with adjustable basket) is far safer than a pan filled with oil over an open heat. This method is used to cook most items including goujons of fish, meat samosas and even deep-fried ice cream.

There are some concerns with deep frying that the food produced is soaked in fat and could pose a risk to general health and subsequently result in a coronary condition.

Coatings

Pane: this is where the product, for example, strips of chicken is passed through flour, egg and then breadcrumbs. The breadcrumbs can be substituted for other ingredients including sesame seeds or oatmeal.

Batter: there are a variety of batters available to coat vegetables, meat and fish including beer batter and tempura.

Shallow frying

Shallow frying is the process of cooking a product in a small amount of hot oil in a shallow pan over an open heat.

Oils

Olive oil gives a Mediterranean flavour and can be raised to a high temperature before burning.

Butter can be used for shallow frying but take care as it burns easily in a hot pan unless clarified. Clarified butter is butter that has been melted slowly and the scum removed from the top and the milk removed from the bottom of the pan. The resulting fat (when warm) is a clear liquid that has the flavour of butter but the properties of oil and can be raised to a high temperature.

Many restaurants have frying equipment

KEY TERM

Stir-fry: a fast method of cooking in a small amount of oil over a high heat while constantly keeping the food moving. Traditionally a round-bottomed wok pan is used.

TRY THIS

If you use a mixture of oil and butter when shallow frying, you get the flavour of butter and the oil stops the butter burning. It has a high temperature before burning.

Recipes

Deep-fried goujons of sole – serves 4

Ingredients:

4 large fillets of sole (free from bone or skin)   10 g yeast
200 g plain flour   Pinch of salt
250 ml beer

Method:

1 Cut the sole into goujons (strips).
2 Make the batter by sifting the flour into a large bowl, adding the yeast and whisking the beer into the flour to make a smooth batter.
3 Add a pinch of salt and adjust consistency if necessary.
4 Pass the sole through the beer batter and cook in the deep fryer at 180°C until golden brown.
5 Take care when putting the fish into the oil not to splash as the hot oil could cause a serious burn.
6 Drain the goujons of sole on kitchen paper and serve with an appropriate garnish.

Pan-fried salmon – serves 4

Ingredients:

4 salmon supreme (free from skin and bone)   1 bunch spring onions
olive oil   small bag spinach
500 g maris piper potatoes   300 ml crème frâiche
100 ml double cream   1 pack chives
25 g butter

Method:

1 Gently boil the potatoes (cut into even-sized pieces), drain and mash.
2 Add the cream, butter and chopped spring onion to taste. Keep warm.
3 Trim the supreme of salmon if necessary.
4 Heat a non-stick pan and place a drop of olive oil into the pan.
5 Place the salmon fillets into the pan, presentation side down and cook for approximately 30 seconds.
6 Reduce the heat and cook the salmon very slowly until the colour changes from translucent to a more whitish finish.
7 Once the salmon fillet seems to be visibly cooked from the base to the top, flip the salmon fillets over and cook for a further minute.
8 Put onto kitchen paper to rest.
9 Gently heat the crème frâiche, add the chopped chives and spinach (stalks removed and washed). A little water or white wine may be necessary to adjust the consistency of the sauce.
10 Wilt the spinach in the sauce for a few seconds and serve with the spring onion mash and salmon supreme.

ACTIVITY

Research the strengths and weaknesses of frying as a method of cookery.

In a group, discuss different uses of oils within frying and state their properties.

KEY TERM

Wilt: soften delicate leaves such as spinach without really cooking them.

CHECK YOUR KNOWLEDGE

1 How can fish be coated before frying?
2 Why coat food prior to frying?
3 Give three examples of food suitable for frying.

8.9 Baking, roasting and grilling

Baking

Baking is a dry heat without any oil or fat, which can be done quite efficiently in a conventional oven. However, in a convection oven (fan assisted), the air is forced around to create a more even distribution of heat and a more consistent end result.

Roasting

Any item that is roasted can either be flash-roasted (blasted in a hot oven and turned down) or sealed in hot oil first and the oven turned down to a long-term cooking temperature.

Pot roasting

As the name suggests, the item is placed in a pot, generally on a bed of vegetables and the lid removed during the final stages to brown the product.

Spit roasting

Whole carcases of meat or poultry can be cooked in this method over an open flame with a rotating centre spit.

Grilling

Most people think that the grill used at home (over the product) is called a grill, when in fact in catering terminology this is called a salamander. This is used for toast, grilling bacon, and so on.

Chargrill

Meat, fish or vegetables are grilled on metal bars over open flames to create a lined effect on the product being cooked, and a distinctive grilled taste.

Barbeque

A similar effect is achieved to chargrilling with a whole range of different barbeques available on the market.

Griddle

A griddle pan is like a heavy frying pan with a ridged base that gives food the look and taste of a barbeque. However food does not have the distinctive barbeque flavour.

Food cooked in a griddle

Recipes

Baked ham shank – serves 4

Ingredients:

4 ham shanks
50 gms Dijon mustard
100 gms Demerara sugar
4 sprigs of fresh thyme

Method:

1 Using the ham shanks that have been previously cooked in the boiling section, place on a greased baking tray.
2 Brush with the Dijon mustard and sprinkle with the chopped fresh thyme.
3 Dust with the Demerara sugar to ensure an even coating
4 Bake in a hot oven for 5 minutes (200°C/gas mark 6)
5 Turn down to 180°C gas mark 4 and cook until fully heated through and the outside is golden brown.
6 Serve with an appropriate garnish.

Roast leg of lamb – serves 4

Ingredients:

1 leg of lamb (boned, rolled and tied)
olive oil
1/2 pack fresh rosemary
1 carrot (large)
1 onion (large)
2 sticks of celery
1 leek
2 tsp tomato puree
2 tbsp plain flour
1/2 bottle white wine
2 litres brown stock

Method:

1 Seal the leg of lamb in hot oil and remove from the pan.
2 Cut all of the vegetables into a mirepoix and sweat in the hot oil.
3 Add the chopped rosemary and place the lamb on the top of the vegetables.
4 Drizzle with olive oil and cook at 180°C or gas mark 4 for 25 minutes per 500 g plus 20 minutes.
5 Remove lamb from the tray and place onto chopping board.
6 Allow lamb to rest. This will tenderise the meat and facilitate carving.
7 To make some gravy, pour away the majority of the fat. Add two tablespoons of plain flour and cook to a roux.
8 Add two teaspoons of tomato purée and stir vigorously.
9 Add the liquid bit by bit to make a rich gravy.
10 Boil gravy to achieve correct consistency.
11 Strain and serve with slices of the roast lamb.

ACTIVITY

You have been given the job of grill chef at the local restaurant. Your task is to select a range of suitable cuts of vegetables, meat and fish that customers would find appealing and suggest appropriate accompaniments. For this task, you may use the internet and books.

CHECK YOUR KNOWLEDGE

1 What is pot roasting?
2 Why baste meat while it is roasting?
3 Why do chefs chargrill food?

117

8.10 Soups and sauces

Sauces

Whether a dish is meat, fish, poultry or vegetable and the time of day or occasion, might dictate the type of sauce to accompany it. Here are a selection of available sauces:

- roux-based, for example, béchamel or veloute
- cream-based, for example chive and lemon
- reduction sauce, for example, redcurrant
- tomato-based sauce, for example, tomato and oregano
- gravy or jus
- cold sauces, for example, mayonnaise or vinaigrette.

The main thing to consider when making a sauce is how it will complement a dish. For example, a delicate lemon and dill sauce might complement a sole dish but would be a disaster with a T-bone steak.

Consistency is a big factor because no customer wants a gloopy or overly thick sauce smothered all over their food.

Roux-based sauces

A roux is a combination of fat and flour cooked to a particular degree, depending on the sauce. The example below uses a white roux with milk as the liquid. To make a veloute, just cook the roux a little more and instead of using milk, use a white stock.

Mornay sauce (cheese)

Ingredients:

400 ml full-fat milk	1 bay leaf
25 g butter	black pepper
25 g plain flour	cayenne
75 g mature cheddar	

Method:

1 Put the butter in a medium saucepan and melt it over a low heat.
2 Add the plain flour and stir to a thick paste.
3 Cook the roux without browning.
4 Gradually add the milk to the roux, taking care not to add too much at a time.
5 Incorporate all of the milk, making a smooth sauce with no lumps.
6 Add the bay leaf and turn down to a simmer for five minutes.
7 Keep stirring to stop the sauce from catching on the bottom.
8 Add the cheddar cheese.
9 Season the sauce well with black pepper and a pinch of cayenne.
10 Only add salt if necessary because the cheese will contain a certain amount of salt already.
11 Remove the bay leaf.

Soups

Soups are a personal preference, you may like chunky or smooth, spicy or tomato, then there are multitude of soups to choose from. Here are just some of the types of soup and an example:

- veloute: (mushroom and oregano)
- cream: (tomato and basil)
- purée: (carrot and coriander)
- broth: (scotch broth)
- chowder: (clam)
- bisque: (lobster)
- national soup: (minestrone or borsch)
- cold soup: (gazpacho)
- brown soups: (mulligatawny or oxtail)
- consommé: (game).

Carrot and coriander soup – serves 4

Ingredients:

25 g butter	1 potato
1 onion	4 sprigs fresh coriander
3 carrots	1 vegetable stock

Method:

1 Melt the butter in a medium saucepan.
2 Cut the onions roughly (mirepoix) and sweat in the butter.
3 Add the roughly cut carrots and chopped fresh coriander.
4 Add cubes of potato. Sweat without colour until tender.
5 Add half the vegetable stock.
6 Simmer for 15–20 minutes.
7 Add more liquid if required.
8 Liquidise and correct consistency.
9 Season with salt and black pepper.
10 Take care not to over-season as the stock may contain salt.

FIND OUT

You have taken delivery of lemon sole and wish to develop a dish for the specials board. Using the internet and cookery books, find a suitable sauce to accompany this fish.

CHECK YOUR KNOWLEDGE

1 What is a roux?
2 Why is the consistency of a sauce important to the customer?
3 Name three different soups that may be available to customers for lunch in a large hotel.

ACTIVITY

You are in charge of the starter section in a local banqueting facility. Fifty rugby players are due in for lunch and you need to create a suitable soup. Discuss your choice of soup, suggesting reasons for your choice.

8.11 Patisserie and desserts

This is a huge area and encompasses dough, sponges, cakes, pastries, scones, puddings, mousses, rice dishes and many more. Here is a selection to help you investigate this varied and interesting part of the menu.

Dough

From basic bread dough to an enriched dough product such as Chelsea buns, there are a number of dough-related products including:

- brioche (a bread related product heavily enriched with butter and eggs)
- speciality breads such as apricot and walnut
- allergy-related breads, for example, gluten-free or spelt bread (for those with wheat intolerance).

These products are generally made from good quality strong flour, which contains a high proportion of the protein gluten, which forms an elasticated structure giving body to the bread.

Pastries

The flour used from pastry is generally soft with a few exceptions to the rule. Different pastries have different textures and different eating qualities and can be used for both sweet and savoury products. Here is a selection:

- puff pastry
- short pastry
- suet pastry
- sweet pastry
- flaky pastry
- choux pastry
- filo pastry.

Puddings

Puddings are broken down into both hot and cold desserts. The table shows just a small sample of available puddings.

Hot	Cold
sticky toffee pudding	rice pudding
jam roly poly	crème brûlée
treacle sponge	raspberry pavlova

Cakes and sponges

There are many different cake recipes available both in books and through the internet. The same recipe can be shown in hundreds of different ways. Here are a selection:

- Christmas cake
- fruits of the forest gateau
- Victoria sandwich
- carrot cake
- coffee and hazelnut Genoese.

Recipes
Basic bread (Chorley Wood)

Ingredients:

Bowl 1	Bowl 2
500 g strong flour	1 tsp yeast
25 g milk powder	half a tsp sugar
half a tsp salt	300 ml tepid water
olive oil drop	half a vitamin C tablet (unsugared)

Method:

1 In bowl 1, mix the strong flour with the olive oil, milk powder and salt.

2 In bowl 2, mix the tepid water, crushed vitamin C tablet, sugar and yeast.

3 Add the liquid from bowl 2 into bowl 1 gradually to form a dough. (Take care not to add all of the liquid initially as the dough might become soggy.)

4 Knead the dough until smooth.

5 Roll the dough into different shapes according to preference and place on a greased tray.

6 Egg wash the bread for a crisp finish or alternatively dust with flour for a soft finish.

7 Prove the bread in a warm place until it doubles in size.

8 Bake the bread at 200°C or gas mark 6 for 10–15 minutes or until the dough is fully cooked.

9 Cool on a wire rack.

Sticky toffee pudding – serves 4

Ingredients:

90 g dates
150 ml water
half a tsp Bicarbonate of soda
25 g butter
90 g castor sugar
1 egg
90 g self-raising flour
half a tsp vanilla essence
150 ml double cream
25 g demerara sugar
black treacle to taste (1tsp)

Method:

1 Bring the water and chopped dates to the boil.

2 Add the bicarbonate of soda and remove from the heat.

3 Cream the butter and sugar and then incorporate the egg.

4 Whisk in the date mixture and incorporate the flour and vanilla essence.

5 Pour the mixture into a lined pudding dish and bake for approximately 30 minutes or until a metal skewer comes out clean at 180°C or gas mark 4.

6 To make the sticky toffee sauce, gently bring the demerara sugar, black treacle and double cream to the boil.

7 Make sure that all of the sauce ingredients are incorporated but the sauce has not been over boiled.

8 Pour over the pudding to serve.

KEY TERM

Egg wash: egg-based liquid used to glaze pastry or other products before baking.

ACTIVITY

It is the opening night of your restaurant 'Chez Nosh'. You are to create a signature dessert that will be featured in all of your advertising. Design the dessert showing the layers, different colours, any accompanying garnishes and an appropriate sauce.

CHECK YOUR KNOWLEDGE

1 Name three different types of pastry that can be used to create different types of dessert.

2 What is gluten?

3 Define the term 'to prove'.

ExamCafé

Exam preparation

Revision checklist

Which exam	Content	What to revise
All for catering	Meat and poultry	You need to know the difference between meat and poultry and be able to list different types. You should know the correct selection and storage of meat and poultry. Knowledge of meat and poultry preparations would be beneficial.
All for catering	Fish	You need to know the quality points of fresh fish and the correct storage procedures. Knowledge of different cuts of fish would be helpful. You need to know different coatings used on fish before deep frying.
All for catering	Vegetables and fruit	Knowledge of different types and categories of fruit and vegetables would be extremely beneficial. You need to know a range of specialist vegetable cuts. You need to know what to consider when purchasing fresh fruit and vegetables.
All for catering	Dairy and eggs	You need to be able to list a range of dairy or milk products. You should know what to consider when buying eggs. You should be able to suggest alternatives to particular dairy products.
All for catering	Dry goods and convenience products	You should have an awareness of available dry goods and convenience products on the market. You should have an understanding of different types of flours and sugars and know some special properties of the different types.
All for catering	Boiling, steaming and poaching	You should know what blanching is and how it is used in the kitchen. You should know the different ways to steam food products. You should understand the difference between shallow and deep poaching.
All for catering	Braising and stewing	You should understand the difference between braising and stewing. You need to understand which cuts of meat and poultry are suitable for braising and stewing.
All for catering	Frying (deep and shallow)	You should understand safety considerations when deep frying food. You need to know the properties of different types of oils and fats used for deep frying.
All for catering	Baking, roasting and grilling	You need to know a range of foods suitable for baking. You need to understand the differences between conventional roasting, pot roasting and spit roasting. You need to have an awareness of different types of grilling.
All for catering	Soups and sauces	You need to know what a roux is and give examples of roux-based sauces. You need to know a range of hot and cold sauces. You should be able to state different types of soups and understand how they are made.
All for catering	Patisserie and deserts	You should be able to state the differences between a basic bread dough and an enriched dough. You should have a working knowledge of different types of pastries, pudding, cakes and sponges.

Activities

This is a practical unit which is supported by theory. For each food area the selection, storage and preparation of food must be considered. An awareness of different cooking processes is important for a range of different food products.

Exam preparation

Use past exam questions to check your knowledge. Most of the questions are about your knowledge and will ask you to apply your understanding to selected questions. Some questions might relate to catering terminology.

Sample question

When purchasing fresh fish, what quality points should be considered? (6 marks)

Sample answer

The following points should be considered when purchasing fresh fish:

- Fish should have plenty of scales (round fish)
- Pink-red gills
- Bright eyes
- It should have a good amount of slime
- The fish should not have sunken flesh
- All sea fish should smell of the sea and not ammonia
- Chilled (ideally in ice)
- Shellfish should be alive

Examiner's tip
If you have practical experience of working with all commodities you will have a better understanding of these types of questions.

9.1 Introduction to food service and styles of service

Today, a food and drink experience is a whole package of the food, drink and ambience of the establishment and the service received. It is vital that the food service team (also known as front-of-house) works with the food preparation team (also known as kitchen brigade) to give a total experience.

Food service

This is the service of foods and drinks (beverages) to customers in an efficient, safe and hygienic way so that they are satisfied. Whatever the type of establishment, it is important that food service staff have knowledge of the following:

Systems:

- where the customer wishes to be served
- what is available to sell to the customer
- the method of ordering the customer's requirements
- what the customer requires and how much – what the customer's expectations are
- how the items are to be served
- when the customer is ready for the items they have ordered
- what accompaniments should be offered
- how the customer is to be billed for the items and service.

Safety and hygiene:

- the safest and most appropriate method to carry and serve food and drink items
- a high standard of personal hygiene and clean working standards
- knowledge of safe temperatures for holding and serving food
- knowledge of safety procedures such as emergency exits.

Styles of service

Types of service were identified in Chapter 1.7. These were divided up into three main methods of table, counter and personal and then subdivided into methods of service. Refer to Chapter 1.7 to remind yourself of these.

The type of service depends on the style of establishment, whether it is a restaurant, café, café-bar, coffee shop, fast-food outlet or public house.

Food and drink outlets

Eating and drinking outlets have been identified in Chapter 1.6. Here, these different outlets will be matched up to styles of service.

CASE STUDY

The Majestic Hotel has three different food service outlets:

1 **Fine dining restaurant** seating 30 people, open evenings only, where there is a half-and-half service. The main part of the meal is plated in a decorative way. Vegetables are served silver-service.

2 **Family bistro** seating 100 people open 11am–11pm. All meals are plated and include vegetables.

3 **Banqueting rooms** that can seat up to 200 people. Service varies, it can be:
 a buffet style where guests help themselves to a variety of finger-foods
 b buffest style where the food service staff serve guests with a variety of fork food
 c carvery service where a chef cuts and serves roast meats and guests help themselves to vegetables
 d sit down meal where all the food including the meat is silver-served.

Restaurants provide food and drink at medium to high prices and give high levels of service in comfortable surroundings.

All service is at the table except for special restaurants, such as a carvery restaurant where roast meat is cut and served, and also at functions when buffets are often used. Service can be:

- **Plated:** the most common type of table service is plated service where the whole meal is served in a creative way.
- **Half-and-half** service can also be partially plated service, where the main part of the meal is plated and vegetables are served family-style – put on the table or silver-service.
- **Family:** this is most suitable for ethnic restaurants where people often share a range of dishes. Food is put on the table and customers help themselves.
- **Silver:** is a more traditional style of service and is usually found in the dining restaurants or hotels. Guéridon service can be part of this style of dining, where some dishes are cooked in front of the customer.

Food service is an important part of the industry

Different levels of skill are needed in serving these styles of service. Also, different ratios of staff to customer are needed. Placing a plate onto a table is an easier skill and takes less time than silver-service.

Cafés are usually small, inexpensive places that serve food and drink and can be found in nearly all villages, towns and cities. They serve meals and snacks, including breakfast, during the day. These meals will be plated. Some cafés ask customers to order at the counter, others take orders from the table.

Café-bars serve alchoholic drinks and are open in the evening. They might serve a wider choice of food but this will still be plated.

Coffee shops focus more on serving drinks than food. These outlets usually have a counter-cafeteria style of service, where customers order and collect their food and drink from one service point.

Fast-food outlets are found everywhere and are often open 24 hours a day. Fast food is served with a counter-cafeteria style and can include a takeaway service.

Public houses are a British tradition and in the past only served drinks. Nearly all pubs now serve food, usually plated with a basic table setting. Gastropubs are a new style of food and drink outlet. They are really a more relaxed and less formal restaurant.

Hotels often provide a wide range of eating and drinking experiences for individuals and groups of people, such as for functions like conferences and banquets. Large hotels often have more than one restaurant and can even have a fine dining restaurant, ethnic restaurant and a café-bar. Here you see all styles of table service as well as counter – usually buffet – service.

ACTIVITY

Write a job advert for a food and drink service person in a café and in a hotel restaurant where silver-service is used. Write a description of the skills needed for each job.

ACTIVITY

Give an example of a situation where a food and drink server can show off their serving system and safety and hygiene skills.

CHECK YOUR KNOWLEDGE

1 How many different types of outlet might used a plated style of service?
2 What is the difference between a café and a coffee shop?
3 What is a gastropub?

9.2 Preparing for service

Food service staff don't just turn up when the restaurant or café opens. They have to prepare for service. They have to be organised so that customers have the best experience in the eating or drinking establishment.

For some places, such as a coffee shop, this might mean to check the cleanliness of the place and stock up with the food and drink served behind the counter. For others, it means elaborate table dressing to create the desired theme for a wedding banquet. For all staff, it means understanding the systems and having the safety and hygiene knowledge identified in Chapter 9.1.

Setting up for service

Cleaning

In most establishments, cleaners are employed but it is the responsibility of the food and drink staff to check the cleanliness of the room and know how a room should be cleaned ready for service.

- The room should be cleaned before tables are set.
- The order should be dusting, vacuuming and then mopping – if necessary.
- Windows should be opened to freshen the room.
- Clean clothes should be worn for cleaning.
- Cleaning equipment and chemicals should be stored out of sight of customers.

Laying tables

The style of organising and laying tables depends on the type of outlet.

Tables can be round, square or rectangular. Round ones take up more room but are friendlier to sit at. Some outlets have fixed tables or even booths (these take up the least room). Others have flexible seating that can change daily depending on who has booked.

Table coverings can be as follows:

- Tablecloths are usually made from fabric – usually white but sometimes pastel colours or even a dark or checked colour for ethnic restaurants. They need to cover some of the table legs for good presentation.
- Disposable tablecloths vary from a very cheap banqueting roll to those that look and feel like cloth. Like tablecloths, they are usually white but can be in other colours.

A table cover can be very simple or ornate

- Placemats are often used instead of tablecloths or put on top of the tablecloth for extra colour. They can be fabric, plastic, wood, cork etc, or disposable and can provide colour and interest to a table. If disposable placemats are used, these often advertise the restaurant or local area and often have the menu printed on them. In some outlets, children are given placemats with activities on them.

Place settings

Cutlery, crockery and glasses need to be placed at each setting. How much of these and where they are placed again depends on the type of establishment and the number of courses the customer will be eating. Some establishments have the minimum cutlery on the table and staff add cutlery during the meal, depending on what has been ordered, for example, soup or fish. A large plate can be used to guide where cutlery needs to go on a table when setting it up.

Napkins

| Fan | Bishops hat | Lily | Cone |

Different styles of folding napkins can be found in specialist books or by searching the internet.

As seen in the photos above, napkins can be simply folded in half and placed on the table or folded in different elaborate ways so that this helps to create an ambience or theme to the table.

Flowers and extras

Flowers are used to create the right atmosphere, such as an inexpensive single flower in a vase or a more complicated arrangement.

Condiments are often put on the table. These can simply be salt and pepper, but in a café that serves breakfast might include tomato and brown sauce, vinegar and mayonnaise.

For special occasions, extras are added to tables to create a good colour scheme or theme. Confetti in different shapes or colours can be used together with place names, wedding favours, Christmas crackers, party poppers or mini-presents, such as an individually wrapped chocolate.

ACTIVITY

Design a placemat for a local establishment that shows all the different tourist attractions in the area.

OR

Use a design programme to design a placemat with activities for young children.

TRY THIS

Research different styles of folding napkins. Try out at least three different styles that could be used for a Valentine's day meal.

ACTIVITY

Create on paper an ideal table setting for either a children's party or a Chinese meal.

CHECK YOUR KNOWLEDGE

1 How do you freshen up a room before service?
2 What are the three types of table covering that can be used?
3 What are the three things that need to be placed at a table setting?

9.3 Welcoming guests

When customers enter a food and drink establishment the surroundings – how the room is set up ready for service – is important but even more important is the appearance of the staff and how they serve you.

Personal presentation

Any hospitality worker who interacts with customers must have excellent personal presentation. This includes cleanliness: clean hair and hands, fresh breath and no body odour. They also need smart clothes with suitable footwear and good posture. Staff should wear an absolute minimum of jewellery.

A professional attitude is also needed. Staff should show positive body language, be attentive, not look bored and have good communication skills. (See Chapter 10 for more on this subject.)

Safety and hygiene

All staff working in a food and drink environment are required by law to work safely and maintain correct hygiene standards. Hygiene and safety have been covered in Unit 3 but the following points are worth revising for food and drink service:

- Opening and closing doors: it is best to have an in and out door to the kitchen.
- Carrying trays: these help to reduce work but must not be overloaded as they then create work.
- Dealing with spillages and breakages: spillages must be cleared up immediately and breakages dealt with carefully so that you avoid cuts.
- Safe handling of food and drink: an understanding of high-risk foods and hot and cold holding temperatures is needed for this.
- Safe storage of items: large items such as chairs, trolleys and tables must be stored so they do not fall over. Crockery must not be piled high as it is heavy, and glasses stored so they do not fall and break.
- Clean work areas: these are often on view to customers so must be kept tidy to allow the system to work as well as to support safety and hygiene procedures.

Arrangements like this are a threat to both safety and hygiene

Greeting customers

Customers need to be treated considerately if they are to come back. Welcoming them with a 'good morning', 'good afternoon' or 'good evening' is important as well as, if you know them, by their name. Customers need to be greeted at the door if the establishment has table service. They then need to be shown to their table.

Menus

Menus provide the customer with information about what food and drink they can buy in the venue, a list of items available. By law, menus must be displayed near the entrance to an establishment so that customers can see what is available and the cost before they go in. Menus can be simple – on a chalk board, or above the counter, with photos of dishes to identify items, or can be elaborate booklets that include detailed descriptions of each dish.

This depends on how many different dishes are served as well as the type of establishment.

Examples of different menus can be found on page 88.

Staff can provide extra information to add to that on the menu. This could be what the chef recommends, what is on special offer and what accompaniments suit certain dishes. They should have a detailed knowledge of the menu, what ingredients are in each dish and how it is made. When menus are changed daily, chefs will give briefings before service to inform staff about the dishes. Some customers will be very clear what they want to order but others will need advice and guidance.

Up-selling

Up-selling is used in both food and drink establishments and is a subtle sales method to get customers to spend more money.

For example:

> 'Would you like a side order of onion rings with your steak, Sir?'
> 'Would you like to upgrade that order to a large meal for an extra 50p?'
> 'Is that a large glass, Madam?'

Good up-selling does not allow the customer a free or cheaper alternative. An example of this is the selling of bottled water. If you are asked: 'Is it a sparkling or still bottle of water, Sir?' you are likely to say one or the other not 'No, just a jug of tap water please'. But, if you were asked: ' What kind of water would you like?' you could easily answer: 'A jug of tap water will do.'

Taking orders

Orders can be taken:

- electronically on a handheld computer terminal – the order is shown in a screen or printed out in the kitchen
- in duplicate – one to the kitchen and one kept by the restaurant
- in triplicate – one for the kitchen, one for the restaurant and one for the cashier to complete the bill.

9.4 Table service

Some people go to eating establishments just to stop hunger. Workers go to a canteen to fill themselves up. Children go to a school canteen to give them energy to continue with afternoon lessons.

However, most people go to eating establishments not just to eat but to enjoy the whole social experience.
Part of this is the skill in the way the food is served.

Serving skills

Counter service often requires staff to plate-up the food requested but needs no other serving skill.

At the table, plate service requires less skill than silver-service.

Plate service can sometimes be food simply plated in the kitchen for ease of serving and then placed in front of the customer, such as in a guesthouse. Or meals can be elaborately presented by the chef in a fine dining restaurant and served on a plate so that the presentation is not spoilt.

Food and drink service staff need the skill of carrying hot plates – sometimes three or four and knowing that they should:

Serve from the left (except coffee and tea) and take way from the right.

Plate service

In addition, silver-service staff need to know how to serve food using a spoon and fork and how to serve large and small pieces of food. They need to learn and practice the hand-hold of the spoon and fork so that they can serve a variety of items.

These staff also need to learn about the different cutlery required for different dishes, as they are likely to add these to the table at each course. Often, they will also need to know how to crumb down the table after the main course.

Silver-service

Communication and teamwork

This has already been discussed in Chapter 6. It is particularly important that food and drink service staff communicate well with customers, as well as with kitchen staff – both written and verbally – to meet customer satisfaction. Teamwork is also important so that food is prepared and served on time to meet this satisfaction level.

TRY THIS

Practice serving frozen Brussels sprouts or peas and bread rolls to develop your silver-service technique.

Timing

An important skill that staff need is being aware of time. Knowing how long a customer has been waiting for:

- a table
- the order to be taken
- the food to arrive
- a menu
- their drinks to arrive
- their bill.

Table service tasks

The summary of tasks shown in the table below can be used to train new staff in a restaurant or hotel or be used to remind part-time staff of the system they must follow.

Task	Method	Detail
1 Personal presentation	Wash hands.	Complete appearance.
2 Finish tables	Is water ready? Butter?	Turn up glasses.
3 Greeting	Welcome. Take coats.	Smile, greet, ask if customer has booked.
4 Seat	Escort to table. Meet initial needs.	Assist. Offer menus, drinks, butter, bread, water?
5 Take order	Check pad. Copy to kitchen. Copy for billing.	From host? Suggest. Sell. Write clearly. Confirm – repeat order. Change cover – cutlery.
6 Serve	Plated meals.	From left, serve cold food first, ladies first. Accompaniments? Ask – are customers happy with everything?
7 Clear	Clear each course.	All finished. Make ready for next course. Crumb down table after main course.
8 Serve	Serve coffee etc.	From right, coffee with milk or sugar?
9 Take payment	Check bill, then present.	To host, return to collect or at till. Take payment.
10 Farewell	Assist return of coats. Wish them goodbye.	Check for forgotten items.
11 Re-lay	Prepare for next customers.	
12 Clear	Prepare area ready for next use.	Clear till, record takings. Food returned.
13 Debrief with food preparation staff	Look at problems, complaints and compliments.	Plan how to improve.

If these tasks were for a specific function, extra detail could be added that would show what needs to happen for each course. Part of this might include:

- Clear fish course and lay meat plates.
- Take out dirties and collect potato and other vegetable dishes.
- Deposit on sideboard.
- Collect meat from kitchen.
- Serve to table.
- Serve potatoes and vegetables.
- Leave room taking dirty silver.

9.5 Drink service

Staff who work in drink service sales areas need special skills. The skills depend on the type of drink service establishment. These vary from coffee houses that serve mostly hot beverages, where the skills of a barista are needed, to bars that specialise in alcoholic cocktails, where the skills of a mixologist are required. All drink service staff need to have high levels of communication skills and personal presentation.

Hot beverages

These are served in a variety of establishments including hotels, cafés and pubs as well as coffee shops and café-bars.

Wherever hot beverages are served, staff should be knowledgable about what is available and have the skill to serve them all.

Coffee

This can be made with instant or ground coffee beans. Coffee beans grow on trees, and are dried and roasted. The taste and flavour of coffee depends on how long it has been roasted. There are four main roast types: mild, medium, strong and expresso. There are two main bean types, Robusta and Arabica – these determine flavour too. There are many different coffee drinks as shown in the diagram below.

The skill of a barista

In the UK, the term 'barista' means someone with a level of expertise in preparing expresso-based coffee drinks. In some places, the meaning is expanding to include what might be called a 'coffee sommelier'; a professional highly skilled in coffee preparation with a comprehensive understanding of coffee; coffee blends, expresso, quality, coffee varieties, roast degree, espresso equipment and maintenance, latte art, and so on.

CASE STUDY

Training a Caffè Nero barista takes one week, of which the majority is taken up by learning how to make the perfect espresso and recognising when it is not right. As you see in the illustration, the production of a perfect espresso is the result of a number of different stages. If any one of the stages from the bean, grind, tamp and pour is not perfect, the resulting espresso will not be correct.

Once a barista has learned how to make perfect espresso, they then have to learn all of the different coffee recipes. A Caffè Nero barista spends two days learning how to make the perfect espresso before he or she is allowed to work behind a bar. They then spend a further five days being trained by a 'maestro' before they are allowed to serve a customer on their own (provided they pass the necessary tests). You will recognise trainee baristas in Caffè Nero because they wear a grey t-shirt. They are only allowed to wear the black t-shirt when they have completed their training.

Tips for serving coffee:

1 Coffee must be hot and not too strong or too weak.
2 Serve with hot milk or cream.
3 Serve demerara sugar and possibly a small biscuit.
• Why have barista jobs increased dramatically over the last 10 years?

Tea

This can be served in tea bags or loose in pots. Tea is grown on trees. The leaves are fermented:

- Black tea is fully fermented.
- Oolong tea is semi fermented
- Green tea is not fermented.

There are also tea 'infusions' – any drink that has boiling water poured onto it. These can be:

- herbal such as camomile or raspberry leaf
- fruit such as strawberry and kiwi
- black tea with fruit or flower added to it, such as Earl Grey or jasmine tea.

Tips for serving tea:

- It must be made with boiling water.
- If served with milk it should be cold. Sugar should be white.

Hot chocolate

The cocoa bean also grows on trees and is fermented before being ground. Chocolate drink can be from a commercial mix or from cocoa powder, sugar and hot milk. It can be served with whipped cream and/or marshmallows.

Alcoholic drinks

Wine

Wine is an alcoholic drink made from grapes and is often served with food in restaurants. You looked at the skills of a sommelier in Chapter 2.3. Different types of wine can be drunk on their own but are often served with different foods:

- Red: with red meats, pasta and strong-flavoured foods like game and cheese
- Rosé: with white meats and pasta
- White: with fish and shellfish
- Sweet white: with desserts
- Sparkling: with desserts.

Cocktails

Today, more drink service establishments serve **cocktails**. Often there are specialist cocktail bars that employ trained **mixologists** – a person who creates cocktails. They not only have skills in what to mix but also how to mix, such as free pouring of measures and juggling. This is called flair bartending.

Non-alcoholic drinks

These include bottled water, juices, lemonade and other sweetened fizzy drinks, such as Coca-Cola. Fruit or vegetable-based smoothies are increasingly popular. Juice or smoothie bars are also on the increase.

FIND OUT

Research different coffee shop menus and compare the different coffee drinks on offer.

TRY THIS

Create several different types of hot chocolate drinks and test them for customer satisfaction.

KEY TERMS

Cocktail: an iced drink of wine or distilled liquor mixed with flavouring ingredients.

Mixology: the art of combining various ingredients to make cocktails.

TRY THIS

Experiment with different smoothie recipes to produce a range of smoothies that could be served in a bar.

CHECK YOUR KNOWLEDGE

1 How is a barista trained?

2 What types of tea are available?

3 What is a mixologist?

4 What is a smoothie?

9.6 Acceptable standards in food and drink service

Previous chapters in this unit have discussed the skill and level of service required before, at the beginning and during service. To create total customer satisfaction, staff also need to be skilled in responding to enquiries, dealing with complaints, looking after people with special needs and presenting the bill.

Responding to enquiries

This has partly been discussed in Chapter 6.3 and is all about having knowledge of the system in place in the establishment. Staff should have product knowledge so they can answer any enquiry about the food or drink. They also need to know who to ask – who to communicate with when other enquiries are made. For example – asking the chef for more detail about the menu or asking the restaurant manager about availability tomorrow.

Responding to enquiries is all about personal presentation and communication skills. This means listening and responding politely even if it is to say 'I'm sorry I don't know, I'll find out for you.'

TRY THIS

Visit a local restaurant and assess it for disabled access.

Dealing with complaints

This is discussed in detail in Chapter 10.3. It is important to understand that you cannot deal with all complaints by giving customers their money back – giving them free food and drink. It is important to apologise and deal with the problem. It is important to keep the customer informed about what is happening or what has been done. Perhaps there is a delay in the kitchen – something got burned during cooking or there has been a build up in orders. Customers need to be informed and perhaps a starter or a free drink could be served, to try to prevent complaints.

Special needs

People have different special needs. For example:

Allergies

Someone who is a coeliac – who cannot eat any food containing gluten – has a special need. So staff need to have knowledge of what each dish contains for this and other allergies such as nut and dairy. They need to know about hidden ingredients such as flour to thicken sauces, fish sauces used in curries and milk powders in cake mixes so that customers do not suffer a reaction to the food.

Not all complaints should be solved by giving customers free food or drink

Type of food	What to look out for
Peanuts	These can also be called groundnuts (groundnut oil can be used). They are found in many foods, such as sauces, cakes and desserts. They are also common in Thai and Indonesian dishes.
Nuts	People with nut allergies can react to many types of nut, including almonds, walnuts, Brazil nuts, hazelnuts, pecans and cashews. They are found in many foods, such as sauces, desserts, crackers, ice cream and bread. Ground almonds are used in marzipan.
Gluten	People who have coeliac disease have a gluten intolerance. They need to avoid cereals such as wheat, rye and barley and foods such as bread, pasta, cakes, biscuits and pastry. Wheat flour is also used to thicken sauces and soups. Some foods are dusted with flour before cooking and foods coated in breadcrumbs or batter also contain wheat.
Eggs	Eggs are used in many foods such as cakes, mousses, sauces, pasta and quiche. Eggs are also used to bind ingredients together such as in a burger. They are also used as an egg wash to stick breadcrumbs to a product. Don't forget that egg is used in salad dressings such as a Caesar dressing and mayonnaise. Egg is also used to glaze products.
Fish	Some types of fish, especially anchovies, are used in salad dressings (Caesar), relishes and sauces (Worcester). Also on pizzas. Fish sauce is commonly used on Thai dishes.
Shellfish	People who are allergic to shellfish need to avoid all types, including prawns, scampi, crab, mussels and oysters. Again, Thai and Chinese dishes often use shrimp pates and oyster sauce.
Soya	Soya comes in many different forms: Tofu (a bean curd, soya flour and TVP) textured vegetable protein. It is found in many foods, including meat products, as a cheap bulking ingredient, and in many vegetarian products.
Milk	People with a milk allergy need to avoid foods containing milk, yoghurt, cream, cheese and butter. Some food products are glazed in milk or contain dried milk powder.
Sesame seeds	Sesame seeds are often used to decorate bread and breadsticks. Tahini – sesame seed paste used in the dip Hummus – is a dish from Eastern Europe and the Middle East. Sesame oil is used in cooking, often for Oriental dishes.

Mobility problems

Staff also need to know how to deal with people with mobility problems – either with a walking stick or in a wheelchair. They need to know how to communicate with them correctly, as well as how to help them out in particular situations. For example:

- removing a chair from a table and making sure there is enough room for a wheelchair as well as other guests to walk past
- placing a walking stick so that staff and other guests do not fall over it
- placing the guest at a table that has easy access to the toilet and emergency exits
- helping them with the service of food in a counter situation – can they see all the food available or is it too high? Can they reach all the food available? Is it safe for them to serve themselves? And can they get to and from the counter?

Presenting the bill

Customers can get annoyed if they have to:

- wait for the bill too long
- if it is added up incorrectly
- if it is not clear whether a service charge is included.

Staff need to have good timing, good knowledge of the billing system and how it works and an understanding of service charges (see Chapter 11.5) to give customer satisfaction.

CHECK YOUR KNOWLEDGE

1 How should you respond to an enquiry if you do not know the answer?

2 Why is it important to know if someone has a nut allergy?

3 Why could a person with a walking stick cause an accident to staff?

ExamCafé

Revision checklist

Which exam	Content	What to revise
HOS only	Introduction to food service and styles of service	You need to know what systems skills and safety and hygiene skills food service staff need to have You need to be able to match different styles of service with different food and drink establishments.
HOS only	Preparing for service	You need to know what setting up for service means and all the different aspects of this such as table settings and napkins.
HOS only	Welcoming guests	You need to understand the importance of the attitude of staff to customer satisfaction in an eating or drinking establishment. You need to understand the importance of personal presentation, safety and hygiene and menus. You also need to know the right way to welcome guests, take orders and how to up-sell.
HOS only	Table service	You need to understand that the key aspects of table service are serving skills, communication and teamwork and timing. You need to know the type of schedule food service staff follow during meal service.
HOS only	Drink service	You need to know about the special skills in serving drinks and what types of hot beverages and alcoholic and non-alcoholic drinks are served.
HOS only	Acceptable standards	You need to know how to respond to enquiries, deal with complaints, deal with people with special needs and how to present the bill to achieve acceptable standards of food and drink service.

Activities

The knowledge needed for this unit is learned better if you have practical experience of carrying out preparation, welcoming and serving in a food and drink setting.

Summarising content and exam preparation

Think about the events you have carried out and write down examples of good and bad service you have witnessed.

Sample question

1 Buffet style food service often includes hot and cold dishes.
  a Explain why this is a popular choice for
    i the caterer   (3 marks)
    ii the customer.   (3 marks)
  b Discuss the role of the waiting-on staff in a buffet food
    service system.   (4 marks)

Sample answer

a i Less staff will be needed than table service and the food can
be prepared before the event. It can be quick service and is
less formal.

ii They can help themselves and decide what they want to eat.
They can pile their plate high or just have a little. It is quick
service and just more relaxed.

b In some buffets the waiting-on staff actually serve the food.
They also keep checking to see if the food runs out and liaise
with the kitchen. They also need to clear the plates from the
tables so the customers can get to the next course. Some
waiting-on staff will also serve drinks to customers during
buffet service.

Examiner says:
Think about all the different meals you have
experienced and use your memories to help
you answer these types of questions.

Examiner says:
This is a classic example of a question that
needs planning before any writing begins.
Jot down bullet points in the margin of the
exam paper to make sure you have enough
information for the four marks on offer.

2 A group of catering students have decided to hold an Italian-themed evening at
school. Explain how the students can create the right atmosphere for the event
if they use their canteen as the venue. *(You may wish to consider table settings,
type of tables and personal service.)*
(8 marks)

Sample answer

The tables could have checked tablecloths on them or if that is too
expensive, banqueting roll can be used and red and green coloured
napkins used to add colour. There could be a wine bottle in the
middle of the table with a candle in it or a red flower in a vase.

The lighting needs to be low so not all the lights used and Italian
music needs to be playing.

Round tables are best because they are more sociable – everyone
can speak to everyone.

If possible, posters or bunting could be hung around the room.

There should be someone to greet guests at the entrance and show
them to their table. They should ask them what drinks they would
like and make sure there is butter, bread and water on the table.

The staff should be polite throughout the meal and make sure they
do not have to wait too long between course and for their bill.

Examiner's tips
This needs planning and the
guidance of what to consider
used in this planning. Practical
experience during your course
will help you answer this type of
question. Think: when we did this,
we though about...

Relate what you did in this type of
event to the question.

Chapter 10

CUSTOMER CARE AND SERVICE STANDARDS

10.1 The importance of customer service

If you wait to be served at a fast-food counter while staff chat, drink tea and ignore you, you will walk out and find somewhere else. If you wait an hour and a half to be served a meal in a restaurant without an apology or information about when the meal is coming, you will not return. These are examples of poor customer service.

People in the hospitality industry need a desire to provide excellent customer service. Their job is to make sure that the customers' needs are met.

Customer service is what an establishment does to meet customer expectations and produce customer satisfaction. As the hospitality industry is all about customers, this service is at the centre of the success of any business.

Customer needs

Customers have expectations that their needs, such as a comfortable bed, plenty of hot water and a tasty meal, will be met. Customer satisfaction is created by meeting needs.

The five main customer expectations are:

- **Value for money** – they must feel that the price paid for goods and services is fair. This does not always mean cheap.
- **Accuracy and reliability** – the service or goods promised should be delivered. If a 100 per cent beef burger is promised, a 'value' burger that only contains 30 per cent beef is not good service. Also, the burger must be the same quality every time it is ordered.
- **Information, advice and help** – because customer service is all about understanding people's needs, customers expect that they will be given information and advice before they even ask for it. For example, they may expect a waiter to describe items on the menu.
- **Problems and complaints dealt with correctly** – despite everyone's efforts, sometimes things go wrong. It is important that staff sort problems out quickly and correctly. This is discussed further in Chapter 10.3.
- **Health, safety and security** – there is a duty of care towards customers within an establishment – see Chapter 3.

Makes the customer want to return

Patient

Sincere

Make a real effort to be helpful

Awareness of customer likes/dislikes

Polite — **Good customer service** — Attentive

Respectful

Smile

Friendly

Eye contact

Know the product

Help customer enjoy experience

Customer service is important for the following reasons:

1. **Returning customers.** By choice, people will not return to an establishment where they were not satisfied with the service. So, one of the main aims of customer service is to satisfy the customer so that they will return. Repeat business – returning customers – means a successful business.

2. **Exceeding expectations.** If this is done, repeat business is more likely. As more people become used to eating, drinking and sleeping away from home, expectations are higher. Satisfying needs is not always enough to get people to return. If customer expectations are exceeded and they have received excellent service, they are more likely to return. This is called 'customer service excellence'.

3. **Growth of the business.** If customers receive a high standard of service and return, they will spend more money at the establishment and tell others about it. This means that the establishment is likely to grow, with more sales of services or goods.

Customers

Different customers have different expectations and needs. It is important to identify different market segments of customers so that you can meet these needs.

Business people:
- might be regular customers
- need to be recognised and remembered
- want service to be quick
- might want office facilities such as internet access.

Families:
- want to feel welcome with children – not a nuisance
- facilities for children
- products suitable for children, such as small portions or a special menu.

Groups:
- often have a tour guide who will know the people and help staff look after them
- but everyone is individual and will have different needs.

Different ages:
- Older people might want a more formal approach.
- Assumptions should not be made about a particular age – young people should be shown respect too.

Gender:
- Females might not want a ground floor room in a hotel.
- Males might want larger portions of food.

Culture:
- A person's culture influences dress codes, the way people are greeted, the food and drink they can consume, religious practices and the position of women in society.

Non-English-speaking customers:
- need pictures or hand signs
- need to be spoken to slowly and clearly.

Special needs:
- physical needs such as in a wheelchair
- dietary needs such as coeliac
- learning difficulties.

ACTIVITY

Imagine that you are in each of the following jobs. List four things a customer might ask for help or advice with: receptionist, concierge, room attendant, conference manager. How might you reply?

ACTIVITY

Identify what special services a hotel could provide for female customers.

CHECK YOUR KNOWLEDGE

1 Give a definition of customer service.
2 Why is customer service important for the hospitality industry?
3 Give examples of how the five different needs can be met.

10.2 Measuring customer satisfaction

Finding out the opinions and views of customers helps an establishment to provide the best customer service. It is important to get this feedback from customers – to measure satisfaction, so that the establishment provides the service customers want and remains competitive. It is important to realise that customers' needs change over time and a business must change too.

Feedback

Feedback from customers can be informal or formal.

Informal

This can be through observation or by speaking to customers.

Observing how customers react to certain situations or simply the running of services can tell you a lot. For example:

- If there is a large queue to check into a hotel, this can cause customer dissatisfaction.
- Sometimes if customers are unhappy, they will make loud comments in the hope that they are overheard and something is done.
- People might look at a menu and walk out because it is too expensive or there is not enough choice for vegetarians.

Customers may make verbal complaints or compliments but these tend to be the people who are very unhappy or very happy. To reach the majority of customers, it is important for staff to ask relevant questions to get realistic verbal feedback. Restaurant staff will ask if everything is alright once food is served and reception staff will ask if everything is satisfactory when guests check out.

Some large hotels have customer service managers whose job it is to chat to guests and make sure that customer service excellence is being delivered.

Formal

Informal feedback is very useful but should not be the only way used to get information about customer satisfaction. More formal written methods of feedback are needed, such as comment cards and questionnaires.

Comment cards are usually quite short and useful for instant feedback. They are often left in hotel bedrooms or handed to customers with the bill in restaurants.

Questionnaires are often sent (via the internet) or given to specific customers in the hope that more detailed information is received.

It is important that these comment cards and questionnaires are well laid out and easy to complete. They should be easy to read and the wording clear so that a customer does not misunderstand the questions. They should include closed questions, which require ticks against their choice of answer.

Formal feedback is easier to evaluate than informal feedback. It can be used to check that standards are being kept but also to measure something specific, like a change in the breakfast service.

Customer Comment Card

(Optional)

Customer Name: _____

Phone Number: _____

Comments or Suggestions? _____
_____
_____
_____

	Survey Item	Service Rating						5	Excellent
1	Accommodation	5	4	3	2	1		4	Very Good
2	Room service	5	4	3	2	1		3	Good
3	Catering and food	5	4	3	2	1		2	Fair
4	Overall service	5	4	3	2	1		1	Poor

Mystery guests

Many large organisations, such as hotel chains, use a special person to check into the hotel or eat at the restaurant as a guest. They will have a checklist of points to comment on, such as the service during check in: Did the receptionist smile and give eye contact? Did they ask if the guest wanted a restaurant reservation, and so on. A mystery guest can provide detailed feedback on the level of service provided by an establishment. Mystery guests usually visit every six months.

Staff feedback

Getting staff to relate customer comments is also important, as this helps to provide an overall picture of service. It is also important to get feedback from staff about standards of service they find difficult or easy to deliver.

Evaluating feedback

It is important to measure customer satisfaction but also to work out what to do with the information gained. Feedback should be used to improve services and goods but also to evaluate procedures to see whether they need changing. Formal feedback can be asked for in such a way that it is clear what information is wanted and what will be done with it. For example, if there is a question about value for money, this will inform the establishment whether they need to change prices.

ACTIVITY

Write a comment card for a fish and chip shop or a questionnaire for a sandwich delivery service. Think carefully about what kinds of feedback such a place might need to find out.

CHECK YOUR KNOWLEDGE

1 What is the difference between formal and informal feedback?

2 What can you learn from observing customers?

3 What is the difference between a comment card and a questionnaire?

10.3 Dealing with problems

> Waiter, there is a fly in my soup!

> Can I have some extra onion rings with this meal?

> That steak was horrible. I am not going to pay the bill.

> The bin hasn't been emptied in the room you have just given to me. And there is dust on the top of the TV!

> The shower head has fallen off while I was having a shower!

These are all examples of problems that can happen in the hospitality industry. No matter how well events and procedures are planned and no matter how well workers are trained, there will always be situations when problems arise.

What is important is how these problems are dealt with. Research shows that only 14 per cent of customers are lost because of dissatisfaction with a product, but 68 per cent of customers are lost if the attitude of staff is seen to be unsatisfactory in responding.

'What do you want me to do about it? It's not my fault' is not the correct way to deal with these problems.

Dealing with complaints

Often, customers who complain are angry and sometimes rude. It is important to remain calm and polite and not to take their anger personally.

Using LAST helps to remember the steps needed when dealing with complaints and problems. It means:

LISTEN
Concentrate on what is being said. Show that you are listening properly with your body language. Ask relevant questions. Ask the customer to repeat what they have said and write it down.

APOLOGISE
Always remain calm, polite and professional. Use the right body language, language and tone. Don't make excuses or blame other people. Stay in control.

SOLVE
Solve the problem or pass it on to someone who can. Deal with it immediately or within a sensible time limit. Tell the customer what you are going to do and when. Follow up the problem if you have passed it on.

THANK
Thank the customer for bringing the problem to your attention. Use the right tone of voice when doing this.

Responses and actions

Most problems and complaints need immediate and short-term responses and long-term action.

Most immediate responses are to listen and apologise, unless there are safety issues in which another response might be needed. Long-term actions are about making sure that the problem doesn't happen again.

It is easier to explain about these different responses and actions using the examples already shown.

1 *'Waiter, there is a fly in my soup!'*
   Immediate: Listen and apologise.
   Short-term: Take the soup away and offer a fresh soup or an alternative starter – possibly free.
   Long-term: Find out why there was a fly in the soup. Are cleaning schedules correct and being followed? Are staff trained sufficiently?

2 *'Can I have some extra onion rings with this meal?'*
   Immediate: Listen and possibly apologise and agree to request.
   Short-term: Order onion rings and return with the time they will arrive.
   Long-term: Retrain staff to inform, advise and suggest items on the menu. Up-selling techniques.

3 *'That steak was horrible. I am not going to pay the bill.'*
   Immediate: Listen and apologise.
   Short-term: Negotiate an amount to pay the customer is happy with and/or pass on the complaint to the manager or supervisor.
   Long-term: Check with the kitchen about the quality of steaks being purchased, as well as the methods of cooking. Check whether further training is needed or a new supplier needs to be found.

4 *'The bin hasn't been emptied in the room you have just given to me. And there is dust on top of the TV.'*
   Immediate: Listen and apologise.
   Short-term: If possible, change the room or get a room attendant to clean the room.
   Long-term: See whether room-checking procedures are in place and being carried out. Retrain staff.

5 *'The shower head has fallen off while I was having a shower.'*
   Immediate: Listen and apologise.
   Short-term: Get it mended if there are maintenance staff available or change the room.
   Long-term: See whether room-checking procedures are in place and being carried out including a regular maintenance check. Retrain staff.

ACTIVITY

What immediate and short-term responses and long-term actions should you make for the following problems?

1 A slug was found in a salad.
2 Different-sized scones were served to a group of four.
3 No towels were left for customers to use in the leisure club.
4 Room service took over an hour to deliver a meal.
5 The newspaper ordered for Room 2 did not arrive.

CHECK YOUR KNOWLEDGE

1 What is the main reason customers don't return to an establishment?
2 Why is it important to remain calm and polite when dealing with a complaint?
3 What is the difference between an immediate response and a long-term reaction when dealing with problems?

10.4 Customer care and personal presentation

Good customer service is about putting customers first and providing fast, friendly and accurate service that customers expect.

Customer care guidelines

The following headings are used in customer care guidelines:

Prepare

- Good personal appearance creates a positive first impression.
- Good product knowledge helps you answer questions and give advice.

Greet

- Make positive eye contact and smile to each customer.
- Be sincere in what you say.
- Treat people as if they were guests in your own home.

Listen

- Listen to the complete order/request. Be patient.
- Use positive body language when listening.

Check

- Clarify or check that you have heard the order/request correctly.
- If you cannot hear – tell them.

Present

- If it's not right, don't serve it.
- Present food in a way that shows care and attention.

Thank

- Acknowledge payment politely using 'please' and 'thank you'.
- Use your own words to thank customers and ask them to come again.
- Use the customer's surname and title if you know it.

These guidelines explain that personal presentation is key to good customer service.

Personal presentation

Appearance, hygiene, body language, attitude and behaviour as well as communication skills and presentation of work areas and equipment are all part of personal presentation and all important ways of presenting a positive image to customers.

Appearance and hygiene

First impressions are really important as there is only one chance to impress. Staff who are smart and presentable are already halfway to impressing customers. Good personal hygiene is part of this presentation. Hair and nails should be clean and tidy. There should not be too much make up or jewellery and staff should wash daily so they do not smell. Underwear should not be visible and clothes should be clean, ironed and not faulty – no dropped hems or missing buttons!

An establishment that is part of a large organisation will usually have a corporate image to help with appearance. They will have a uniform for staff so that everyone is correctly dressed.

Body language, attitude and behaviour

Body language is the gestures, poses, movements and facial expressions that a person uses to communicate. It is often called non-verbal communication and accounts for more than half of the way we communicate. Good body language helps to show a good attitude and appropriate behaviour.

Good body language helps towards showing respect for customers. See Chapter 6.4 for more on this.

Communication skills

Appropriate verbal communication is the other way we show respect to customers. The way we greet customers is one of the most important parts of this communication and helps towards those important first impressions.

Communication is about listening as well as speaking. It is important that you are clear about what has been said but also how it was said. Listening carefully is an important skill to learn.

Speaking correctly is also important. You need to use the right tone and pitch of voice. This also needs to vary to show that you are interested in the conversation. You need to speak clearly and not use slang or jargon, so that people understand you. For more on communication skills see Chapters 6.3 and 6.4.

Presentation of work areas and equipment

First impressions are also formed by the presentation of work areas. If you saw a smart receptionist sitting behind a desk piled high with pieces of paper, you would not get a good impression. Or if you saw a waiter's station piled high with dirty dishes, even though the waiter was smart, this would not create the right image.

TRY THIS

Design a corporate image for a new chain of vegetarian restaurants. Think about different members of staff, how will the corporate image differ in different jobs. Justify your choices.

CHECK YOUR KNOWLEDGE

1 Explain how to listen to customers and why this is important.
2 Why is good personal hygiene an important part of customer care?
3 What is non-verbal communication?

10.5 Standards and quality controls

Customer service standards are set by most establishments. These standards either say what has to be done or said in situations, or describe how to perform a task competently.

For example:

Receptionists wear name badges and have to answer the phone before the fourth ring.

A positive personal image to customers means: treat customers in a courteous manner, maintain standards of appearance and try to be helpful.

What standards are **operational standards**.

How standards are **competence standards**. These give detailed performance criteria on how to do a task. Below are some examples of operational standards.

> **KEY TERMS**
>
> **Operational standard:** what has to be done in a particular situation.
>
> **Competence standard:** how a task should be performed competently.

Activity	Minimum standard to be achieved	When/how it will be checked
Answering the telephone	Answer before three or four rings.	Use mystery guest or manager on a regular basis.
Greeting at reception	Acknowledge customer within about 20 seconds.	Front-office manager or duty manager to check.
Making sure that the toilets are cleaned	Check and clean every hour – with a signature.	Head housekeeper or supervisor to check daily.
Making sure that staff have the right product knowledge	Ensure full training and awareness of the product range.	Manager or mystery guest to ensure.

Measuring standards

These standards are usually written down in the operational and training documents of an organisation. They are ways to measure the quality of customer service. They are levels of quality or achievement that are acceptable and an agreed target to aim for. These standards allow for consistency of customer service – a key part of the quality of that service.

A service audit can be carried out using these standards. A checklist should be used, focusing on a range of standards. It might be graded to provide scores for each standard, as shown below:

Customer care standard	Above standard 3	At standard 2	Not observed	Below standard 0
All customers are greeted as soon as they enter the premises.				
Clean correct uniform is worn.				
Staff speak in a friendly manner while serving.				

National standards

Customers like to know the standards they are likely to get when visiting an establishment. There is a national standard for hotels and guesthouses. This includes standards of customer service as shown below.

Star rating	Hotel	Guest accommodation
*	Courteous staff provide an informal yet competent service. The majority of rooms are en suite, and a designated eating area serves breakfast daily and dinner most evenings.	Minimum quality requirements for cleanliness, maintenance, hospitality, facilities and services. A cooked or substantial continental breakfast is served in a dining room or eating area, or bedroom only.
**	All rooms are en suite or have private facilities. A restaurant or dining room serves breakfast daily and dinner most evenings.	Courteous service, well-maintained beds, and breakfast prepared with a good level of care.
***	Staff are smartly and professionally presented. All rooms are en suite, and the restaurant or dining room is open to residents and non-residents.	Friendly welcome, and good quality, well-presented beds and furniture. A choice of good quality, freshly cooked food is available at breakfast.
****	Professional, uniformed staff respond to your needs or requests, and there usually are well-appointed public areas. The restaurant or dining room is open to residents and non-residents, and lunch is available in a designated eating area.	Attentive, more personalised service. At least half of the bedrooms are en suite or have private bathrooms (from 1 Jan 2008). Very good beds and high quality furniture. Breakfast offers a greater choice, and fresh ingredients are cooked and presented with a high level of care.
*****	Luxurious accommodation and public areas, with a range of extra facilities and a multilingual service available. Guests are greeted at the hotel entrance. High quality menu and wine list.	Awareness of each guest's needs with nothing being too much trouble. All bedrooms are en suite or have a private bathroom (from 1 January 2008). Excellent quality beds and furnishings. Breakfast includes specials/home-made items, high quality ingredients, and fresh local produce.

Information from: http://www.theaa.com/staticdocs/pdf/travelandleisure/hotels/quality_standards_for_hotels.pdf.

More detailed criteria about customer service is also listed:

*** Hotel	****Hotel	***** Hotel
Good guest service, with ample staff to provide a prompt and efficient service without detriment to other service areas at the same time. For example it is unlikely that service of this quality will be provided by a member of staff acting as sole bar-person and receptionist at the same time – depending on likely guest demand. Good social skills and anticipation of individual guest's needs evident in dealings with all guests. All staff demonstrate a positive attitude and a willingness to help. Service, efficiency and technical skills of a good standard.	Very good guest service, giving guests the impression of being well cared for by trained professional and attentive staff. Very good social skills and anticipation of individual guest's needs evident in dealings with all guests. Service, efficiency and technical skills of a very good standard and without detriment to other service areas at any time.	Flawless and unobtrusive guest service, giving guests the impression of being very well cared for by highly trained, professional, proactive and well-managed staff. Excellent social skills and anticipation of individual guest's needs evident in dealings with all guests. Service and efficiency of an excellent standard without detriment to other service areas at any time. Delivered by a structured team of staff with a management and supervisory hierarchy. Some multi lingual staff in hotels with an international market.

Information from: http://www.theaa.com/staticdocs/pdf/travelandleisure/hotels/quality_standards_for_hotels.pdf.

This makes it clear what customers should expect when visiting each grade of hotel.

ACTIVITY

Write customer care standards for an event you might run, such as afternoon tea for the elderly.

CHECK YOUR KNOWLEDGE

1 What is the difference between operational and competence standards?

2 What is a service audit?

3 What is the difference between the customer service standards for a 3-star hotel and a 5-star hotel?

Exam Café

Revision checklist

Which exam:	Content	What to revise
HOS only	The importance of customer service	You need to understand why customer service is important, what customer needs are and that different customers have different needs.
HOS only	Measuring customer satisfaction	You need to know the different ways of getting feedback from customers – formal and informal and how to measure and react to this feedback.
HOS only	Dealing with problems	You need to know how to deal with problems and how to respond and act immediately and in the short and long-term.
HOS only	Customer care and personal presentation	You need to know about customer care guidelines and the importance of personal presentation, including hygiene and appearance as well as body language, attitude and behaviour and communication skills.
HOS only	Standards and quality controls	You need to know the difference between operational and competence standards and how standards are measured. You also need to know about national standards of quality.

Common mistakes

It is important to apply your knowledge when answering questions on customer service and not just write about LAST: listen, apologise, solve and thank. You need to refer to the problem identified.

Another common mistake candidates make is to just say that the customers should get a free meal or a drink. In some situations this is not appropriate and alternative solutions should be used!

Exam preparation

Some definitions and knowledge needs to be learnt in this section for example: LAST and what PGLCPT means. Knowing the difference between informal and formal feedback and the difference between operational and competence standards is also very important.

Using past exam papers will help with exam preparation for questions about customer complaints.

Sample question

1 a What do you understand by the term customer care? (2 marks)
  b A customer complains that the meal was not as described on the menu.
    Explain how the restaurant manager would deal with the complaint. (5 marks)

Sample answer

a This is about making the customer feel important and happy so that they return. It is about putting the customers needs first.

b The manager needs to apologise to the customer and then listen to what they say. They must stay calm and not raise their voice. The manager needs to write down information about the complaint and the customers name and details. They need to explain what they will do and report back to the customer when they have found out more. They need to offer some form of compensation if this is relevant. In the long term they need to discuss with the team why this has happened.

Examiner says:
This is a two mark question. It is easy to think you have answered the question but not to have given enough detail for the full two marks. Make sure that you EXPLAIN your answer.

Examiner says:
This type of question needs to be structured and clearly expressed as already mentioned in the planning and structuring answers section on page 19.

This question has five marks so five points need to be included OR less points with explanations. For example the listening point is clarified to explain that it is important HOW the person listens.

Sample question

2 Customer care and quality service are important in the hospitality and catering industry. Satisfied customers will return.

   a Describe how staff in a restaurant can ensure their customers are happy with the service provided.   (4 marks)

   b Discuss the importance of good customer care in the hospitality and catering industry.   (6 marks)

Sample answer

a Staff must be friendly and polite they must be smartly dressed and attentive with a professional attitude so that customers feel welcomed. They need to be aware when customers need their help and not leave them waiting. If there is a delay with the food they must keep them informed. They should be knowledgeable about the food and what is suitable for different diets. Staff could hand out evaluation forms to check that the service is satisfactory.

b If customer care is bad then people won't come back, business will suffer and the place might even shut down. There are so many places to choose from today that customer care is very important, it has to be extra special so you get repeat business. These customers will tell their friends what a nice place it is and the place will get very busy and make more money. That's all down to good customer care.

Examiner says:
A well rounded answer to this type of question does not focus on one point such as the personal presentation of staff. It would be easy to fill the space on the paper with detailed information about hair, nails, no jewellery, little make up and clean and ironed clothes. But this would not cover enough points to gain full marks.

Examiner says:
Candidates often find these types of questions difficult to answer as they are quite vague. If you recognise discuss as meaning 'what are the advantages and disadvantages of' You can plan your answer to show what happens when there is good customer care and then compare it to bad customer care.

Chapter 11

COSTING MENUS AND EVENTS

11.1 Types of cost

To have a successful hospitality establishment, you need to make a profit. To do this, you need to consider the cost of everything you buy and the selling price of goods and services.

There are many different costs in running a hospitality business. They can simply be divided into material, labour and overhead costs. The following are all costs in running a hotel:

Meat and poultry, flour, flowers, chef's wages, dining room staff wages, hotel manager's salary, cleaning materials, heating the kitchen, restaurant bill pads, cost of new furniture, maintenance of ovens, lighting restaurant, depreciation of coffee machine, soap in the toilet, bar staff wages, cost of new curtains for the restaurant, wine, bottled water.

It is easy to classify these items into the three different types of costs: materials, labour or overheads. Any materials not connected with making products are classified as overheads:

Material costs	Labour costs	Overhead costs
meat and poultry	chef's wages	cost of new furniture
flour	dining room staff wages	maintenance of ovens
restaurant bill pads	bar staff wages	lighting restaurant
wine	hotel Manager's salary	heating the kitchen
bottled water		cost of new curtains for the restaurant
soap in toilet		
flowers		
cleaning materials		

Material costs are usually food costs but can also be drinks and what are called consumables, such as paper napkins and other paper goods such as bill pads.

All wages and salaries are of course labour costs.

Fixed and variable costs

Costs can also be divided into fixed and variable costs. Variable costs are costs that fall or increase depending on the amount of business the establishment does. Fixed costs are not influenced by changes in business. Some costs are always fixed and some always variable. Some are fixed up to a certain point and then become variable. For example, telephone and energy costs would increase if business increased considerably.

Some costs are fixed for some businesses and variable for others. For example, a hotel has fixed building and heating costs. A contract caterer will hire a venue such as a marquee or village hall or even have no venue cost if the event is in a home or workplace.

Fixed costs	Variable costs
annual rent management salaries rates insurance staff benefits: accommodation and food energy: heating and lighting	wages food drink tax

Value Added Tax

Value added tax (VAT) is a tax set by the government and is charged on most goods and services (some, such as children's clothes and some food items are zero-rated – not taxed in this way).

Food is a difficult item to consider with VAT. Food is zero-rated but not catering, entertaining, hot takeaway meals, sweets and other luxury items, and alcohol.

The usual rate is 17.5 per cent but a temporary rate of 15 per cent was fixed by the government in 2008. It must be added to the selling price, and handed over to the government (Customs and Excise).

A business cannot keep the VAT, so it makes no difference to the profit a business makes.

A business can reclaim from the government any VAT it has paid on things it has bought, so VAT does not add to its costs.

For example: If a restaurant bill is £40, the restaurant must add VAT of £7 to the bill and charge the customer £47. It sends £7 to Customs and Excise and keeps £40.

If the restaurant has paid £23.50 for the alcohol served with this meal, it will have paid £3.50 in VAT.

So it actually only needs to pay Customs and Excise £7 minus £3.50 = £3.50.

So:

- VAT is added to most goods and services for sale.
- The customer must pay the total, including the VAT.
- The establishment must pay the VAT portion to the government.
- The establishment can reclaim any VAT they pay to suppliers.

To add VAT to a bill you divide by 100 and multiply by 117.5.

ACTIVITY

List the costs of running a smoothie bar. List them under material, labour and overhead costs.

CHECK YOUR KNOWLEDGE

1 What type of cost is buying new chairs for a coffee bar?
2 What is the difference between fixed and variable costs.
3 What is VAT?

11.2 Calculating costs – food costs

Food costs are a large percentage of total costs in most hospitality establishments. Most establishments set a target budget of 30–35 per cent for food costs. They need to do this to be successful and stay in business.

Because of this, chefs don't just guess how much dishes cost to make, they work it out. They use ICT to help them do this with the help of a dish-costing spreadsheet.

Costing dishes

Below is an example of a spreadsheet that uses formulas to quickly work out the cost of a recipe. This helps chefs to calculate the selling price.

The formula used in the actual cost columns is:

the cost of the food bought (per 'packet') divided by the weight of the food bought, multiplied by the weight in the recipe.

On a spreadsheet, the formula will look like this for one row:

= D12/C12*B12

The row number changes each row (e.g minced pork is row 1). The column letters are shown.

DISH: Meatballs	B	C	D	E
Ingredients	Grams in recipe	Weight of food bought	Cost of food per packet	Actual cost
minced pork	450	1000	4.80	2.16
minced beef	450	1000	4.50	2.03
breadcrumbs	200	1000	0.80	0.16
eggs	2	6	0.75	0.25
onion	300	1000	0.74	0.22
green pepper	200	200	0.65	0.65
chicken stock	500	5000	3.00	0.30
white wine	500	3000	9.00	1.50
tomatoes	450	450	0.35	0.35
salt	1	500	0.30	0.00
pepper	1	100	1.00	0.01
nutmeg	1	100	1.00	0.01
parsley	50	35	0.58	0.83
garlic	2	10	0.25	0.05
oil	100	1000	6.00	0.60
tomato puree	25	300	0.51	0.04
			TOTAL COST=	9.16
			NUMBER OF PORTIONS	12.00
			COST PER PORTION	0.76

The portion cost can easily be calculated by dividing the total cost by the number of portions the recipe makes. In this case it is 12 portions.

In this example the formula is: = E20/E22

The selling price is then calculated by dividing by 3 and multiplying by 10. So the selling price is £2.53 if the food budget is 30 per cent.

Chefs will use trade journals, magazines, suppliers' price lists and catalogues to find out the cost of the ingredients they want to use. For small businesses, who do not necessarily buy in bulk and don't get discounts in prices for this, supermarket websites could be used.

Costing menus

A lot of restaurants offer a **table d'hôte** menu that has one set price. There is a choice of a few (two to four) dishes for each course. A chef will have to work out the price for this menu. The chef will do a dish costing for each item and end up with costs like the ones below.

If the chef just takes an average for each course, the cost will be calculated as follows:

Starters	35p	+ 25p	+ 50p	= £1.10	÷ 3		= 37p
Main courses	£1.20	+ £1.30	+ 95p	+ 75p	= £4.20	÷ 4	= £1.05
Vegetables							35p
Desserts	30p	+ 35p	+ 25p	+ 65p	= £1.55	÷ 4	= 39p

The total average cost of a meal is then: £2.16.

Customers preferences

Of course customers may not order to these averages! If you look at the menu, there are likely to be far fewer people ordering the vegetable risotto and the roast beef will probably be the most popular. If cheese is ordered by over half the customers, this would also alter the average cost. Some chefs will use their experience and alter the average cost of the meal to take account of usual customer preferences.

In the example above the average food cost might be increased to £2.40

MENU 1	
Starters	*cost per portion £*
Melon	0.35
Vegetable soup	0.25
Pâté	0.50
Main courses	
Salmon with a prawn sauce	1.20
Roast beef	1.30
Spicy pork casserole	0.95
Vegetable risotto	0.75
Vegetables	
Selection	0.35
Desserts	
Apple and peach crumble	0.30
Plum tart	0.35
Chocolate mousse	0.25
Cheese and biscuits	0.65

KEY TERM

Table d'hôte: a menu at a fixed price.

CHECK YOUR KNOWLEDGE

1 What is a usual food budget for a hospitality establishment?

2 Where would you get information about the cost of ingredients from?

3 Why is it important to take into account customer preferences when calculating the price of a table d'hôte menu?

ACTIVITY

Choose a menu using dishes you have already cooked and use a spreadsheet to calculate the selling price of the menu.

11.3 Cost control

It is important to have a system of controlling costs so that a business stays in profit and continues to operate.

Food

As mentioned in Chapter 11.2, food costs often make up a large proportion of the operating costs of a hospitality establishment. It is important to be in control of these costs.

Foods portioned for cooking and serving

Buying

There are two important procedures for buying:

1. Ordering the correct amount

A chef needs to work out what will be needed over a certain time, taking into account the next delivery date. Stock on shelves not being used costs money as does stock that can no longer be used, such as meat.

2. Ordering the right quality for the right price

The cheapest price is not always the best price. It is important to look for good quality food that is appropriate for that establishment and to use a reliable and reputable supplier who delivers the same quality each week and has very good food hygiene practice.

Using local suppliers will mean that the food is likely to be fresher and a better quality.

Specialised equipment for portioning food

Stock control

The system of first in first out – FIFO – should be followed so that wastage is kept to the minimum, especially for perishable goods.

To help with the ordering of the correct amount and to control costs, a computerised food and beverage management system is often used. The system will automate stock control, ordering, purchasing and requisitions. This kind of system can also be linked to other systems, such as point of sale touch-screen terminals.

Preparation controls

Recipes help chefs to produce food to consistent standards and in consistent quantities. This allows chefs to accurately cost dishes. Recipes also help with ordering the correct quantities.

The correct weighing and measuring equipment needs to be provided during food preparation and serving so that costs are controlled.

Electronic weighing scales, measuring spoons and jugs should be used as well as ladles, scoops and individual or portioned pie dishes. These are all examples of portion control.

Some wastage is inevitable in a kitchen. This needs to be taken into account when working out food costs but does need to be controlled. Skilled staff help to reduce costs by not making mistakes – for example, by overcooking fish or curdling custard. Skilled staff will also be more likely to use the correct ingredients and use all of the ingredients available, for example, a whole chicken – the breast for one dish, the legs for a curry and the carcass for soup.

Budgets

As most hospitality establishments set a target budget of 30–35 per cent for food costs to remain profitable, all the above controls will help an establishment to meet this budget.

Within the food budget will be a food wastage target budget. If food wastage runs at £20 a day, that is £140 a week and £7,300 a year. If food wastage rose by just £5 to £25 a day, that would almost cost an extra £2,000 a year.

Labour

Labour costs – wages and salaries – make up another large proportion of the operating costs of a hospitality establishment. It is important to be in control of these costs. Again, most establishments will have a wage budget that varies depending on the type of operation it is. For example, a 5-star hotel will have a higher wages budget than a fast-food outlet.

Labour costs are more of a fixed cost than food so careful planning is needed to get the balance right so that the level of service is consistent. For example, two waiters might be needed during the week in a restaurant but when it is busy at the weekend, four people might be needed. It isn't economical, and it won't be within budget, to employ four full-time waiters.

CHECK YOUR KNOWLEDGE

1 How can you control costs when buying food?

2 What does FIFO mean?

3 What weighing and measuring equipment can be used to control costs?

4 Why are labour costs difficult to control?

ACTIVITY

Visit a kitchen and write down all the portion control equipment used.

11.4 Calculating profits

Hospitality establishments need to be able to calculate profit margins so that they can check that their business is successful and making a profit. They need to do this regularly. Most large establishments will calculate profits monthly to match up to target budgets.

Establishments need to consider other costs as well as just food costs so that a selling price can be established. They need to first work out gross profit. This then leads onto calculating net profit.

Gross profit

Gross profit is the money that is left when **food costs** have been deducted from the sales income. This helps businesses to check that their target food budgets are being met.

Sales income is all money that is received from customers in payment for food, drinks and services.

If the sales income for a restaurant is £5,750 for a week and food costs are £1,975, the gross profit is £3,775.

If the sales income for a restaurant is £1,640 for a week and food costs are £560, the gross profit is £1,080.

To calculate **gross profit** as a percentage, you:

- divide the gross profit by the sales income
- multiply the answer by 100 to change it to a percentage
    £2,760 ÷ £4,250 × 100 = 65%

To calculate the **food cost** as a percentage, you:

- divide the food cost by the sales income
- multiply the answer by 100 to change it to a percentage
    £1,490 ÷ £4,250 × 100 = 35%.

> **KEY TERM**
>
> **Food cost:** the cost of all the ingredients in all the dishes served in an establishment.

Net profit

To get a true picture of how much profit a business is making and how much it is really costing to run, other costs need to be included in calculating individual dishes and menus, as well as drinks and services.

Net profit is the money left when food costs, labour costs and overhead costs have been deducted from sales income.

Labour costs are the cost of employing the various types of staff needed by the establishment. These can be direct, such as a chef's wage, and indirect, such as a hotel manager's salary.

Overheads are the amounts spent on other items not classed as materials or labour. These include rent, council tax, water rates, gas, electricity, telephone, maintenance and repairs, advertising and marketing and sundry items such as cleaning materials and napkins, and so on.

Over a year, a restaurant business took £155,750 in food and drink sales. Its total food costs were £54,500, labour costs were £46,700 and overhead costs were £31,150. So its net profit was £23,400.

To calculate the net profit as a percentage you:
- divide net profit by the sales income
- multiply the answer by 100 to change it to a percentage.

Proportioning costs

Sometimes, to help get a true picture of how much a business is costing to run, a proportion of the labour and overhead costs are included when calculating the cost of individual dishes and menus. To do this, you:
- work out the number of individual portions sold in a week
- divide the number of portions by the labour costs and overhead costs.

This gives an average cost per portion.

If records are kept of the number of portions of all the different dishes sold, then the total number of portions in a week can be found out.

If 500 portions are sold in one week and labour costs for the week are £1,125, the average labour cost would be:

labour costs divided by individual portions = labour cost per portion

1125 ÷ 500 = £2.25

If 500 portions are sold in one week and overhead costs for the week are £815, the average overhead cost would be:

overhead costs divided by individual portions = overhead cost per portion

815 ÷ 500 = £1.63

If you had already calculated the food cost of an item as £2.55, the total cost would be £6.43.

If your target was 20 per cent net profit, you can calculate the selling price of this item by:

dividing the total cost by 100 and multiplying by 120.

6.43 ÷ 100 = 0.0643 × 120 = £7.72

All these calculations will help a business to remain in profit and continue to exist.

TRY THIS

Run an event. Work out how much you need to charge if labour costs and overhead costs are included.

CHECK YOUR KNOWLEDGE

1 What is gross profit?
2 What is net profit?
3 What is sales income?

11.5 Break-even points and other information

Break-even point

A business' break-even point is where its total costs equal the total of its sales income.

It is at this point that most businesses can survive.

At this point, the business is neither making a profit or a loss.

If a business wants to work out how many units or sales are needed to make a profit then a break-even point is calculated. The break-even point graph can also be used as a tool to determining prices.

The break-even point of a business is very important because it can show:

- the amount of meals, items or services that need to be sold in order to make a profit
- the price that needs to be charged for goods and services
- how price changes would affect the business' profits.

Here is an example:

Fred has a burger van.
His fixed costs of rent, gas and wages are £400 a week.
He charges £2.50 per burger. His food costs are £1.00 per burger.

$$\text{Break even} = \frac{400}{2.50 - 1} = \frac{400}{1.5} = 266$$

He needs to sell 266 burgers a week to break even.

A better way to show break-even points is to use a graph.

For a small business, there are fixed daily costs of £50, each unit costs £12 (variable costs) and each unit is sold for £20.

The business makes a loss if less than seven units are sold and makes a profit if more than seven units are sold.

To work out a break-even point for a business, you need to know its sales revenue per unit sold, for example, how much a bedroom is sold for.

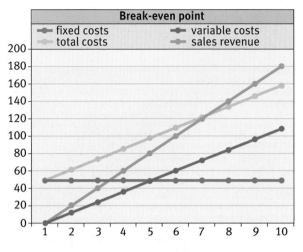

A small business has a break-even point of seven units

Break-even point is three rooms at £75 or four rooms at £50

Using the break-even point to calculate prices

Some businesses use the graph method to work out the price of their goods. A small hotel might work out how much to charge for a room when they can see how many rooms need to be sold in a week to break even.

Discounts and service charges

Discounts are reductions in the price of goods or services to be charged. They are given to different customers for different reasons. Discounts are often given when selling rooms in hotels. Discounts are made to the rack rate – the standard charge for a room. They are often given to businesses and companies who send large numbers of individual or group guests to the hotel. This is often called the corporate rate.

Discounts are also often given to group bookings by tour operators or just private groups. This is often called a tour rate or group rate.

A **service charge** is an amount added to a bill in some hotels and restaurants. It is supposed to be the customer's contribution towards the staff who provided the service. In some establishments, it is passed on to such staff. In many cases, it is just an extra charge and retained as part of the profits of the establishment.

The service charge is mandatory – you have to pay – unless it has been stated on the menu otherwise. It is usually 10–15 per cent.

Service charges are subject to VAT, so should be added to the bill before calculating VAT.

But most hotels and restaurants advertise their prices 'including VAT' and the service charge is simply added at the end.

KEY TERM

Rack rate: the standard charge for a hotel bedroom.

TRY THIS

On a visit to a hotel, ask them about their different room rates.

CHECK YOUR KNOWLEDGE

1 Why would a hotel use a break-even graph to calculate the cost of its rooms?
2 What is a rack rate?
3 Explain the different discounts hotels have for their rooms.

ExamCafé

Revision checklist

Which exam	Content	What to revise
HOS	Types of costs	You need to know that there are material, labour and overhead costs, there are fixed and variable costs and about the cost of VAT.
HOS and CAT	Calculating costs	You need to know how to calculate the cost of food dishes and menus.
CAT and possibly HOS	Cost control	You need to understand the importance of cost control and how costs can be controlled when buying, with stock control, during preparation and with labour. You need to understand how budgets help control costs.
HOS	Calculating profit	You need to know how to calculate gross and net profit and how to proportion costs.
HOS	Break-even points and other information	You need to know how to calculate break-even points and how discounts and service charges could affect these calculations.

Activities

Look at existing menus to be knowledgeable about the prices of dishes sold in restaurants.

Summarising content

Cost is key to the success of a business and evaluating costs is a useful way to work out how successful an event or a business is. You need to understand different costs, how to calculate profits and how to work out break-even points to evaluate successfully.

Exam preparation

Make sure that during the course you have had practice calculating different costs so that you understand the impact reducing certain costs would have for a restaurant, hotel or event.

Sample question

1 Discuss the importance of consistent portion control of desserts to both the customer and the hotel.   (4 marks)

Sample answer

For the customer it means that they all get the same portion for the same price – it is fair and that means they will be satisfied not unhappy.

For the hotel it means there is likely to be less waste and more profit. It means they are controlling costs because they can calculate the portion cost of dishes and work out the correct selling price.

Sample question

2 A hotel/restaurant did not make a profit last year and wants to work out what changes they need to make so that they can make a profit this year. Suggest different ways the hotel/restaurant can improve their profit.
NB – You can choose the type of hotel or restaurant.   (6 marks)

Sample answer

Increase prices.

Reduce other costs such as wages.

Reduce prices to increase volume – if a scone costs 25p instead of 50p – you might sell more than double so that sales are higher.

Increase selling period/time – open for lunch as well as dinner or open for longer.

Cut costs – of ingredients (quality or quantity – you could reduce portion sizes) or labour costs – but would service suffer?

Use marketing techniques:

Advertising – leaflets, posters, paper or magazine adds, Radio or TV adds.

Workers 'up-sell', for example: 'Is that a large one Sir?' or 'Would you like any side orders with that?'

Chapter 12

PLANNING A FUNCTION

12.1 Introduction to the event-based task

The event-based task is a controlled assessment and worth 60 per cent (single award Hospitality GCSE) or 30 per cent (double award Hospitality and Catering GCSE). It is important that the chosen event is investigated and planned in lots of detail and then carried out and evaluated precisely.

Type of event

The event must cater for at least 10 people. It can be one of a variety of possible events such as:

- a charity fundraising event
- a celebration such as Eid, Chinese New Year, wedding or birthday
- an event that a school or college already might host during the year.

Examples of events are:

A birthday party is one of many events you could organise

Charity fundraisers

Organising an event can be an excellent way to raise money for a charity. A wide range of events can be planned, for example a sporting event such as a sportsman's dinner, a fashion show, a coffee morning or a musical evening.

Important things to consider with a charity event are:

- deciding how the money will be raised – through ticket sales, a raffle or an auction (local companies may be willing to support the event by donating prizes or goods and equipment)
- seeing if the charity you are supporting can give you promotional material to help support the event
- making it clear to customers what proportion of the money received will be donated to the charity
- considering the target market – what type of customer is likely to attend the event.

Celebrations

These are social events and can take many forms. For this type of event, the most important thing to consider is whether it is the right event for the guests. Is it the right venue, food and entertainment for the type of guests invited?

Different types of guests might prefer:

- a formal sit-down meal
- a cold buffet
- exotic food
- an afternoon tea
- supper
- a hot buffet
- traditional food
- a lunchtime meal
- an evening meal
- a barbecue.

They might also vary in the type of entertainment they would like:

- a disco
- background music only
- a live band
- no music.

Or:

- party games
- an entertainer such as a clown or comedian.

ACTIVITY

Working in groups, conduct a brainstorm to identify a range of events that you could put on as a group. Record the results on a large sheet of paper. Pick out the most popular ideas using a scoring system.

School or college based events

These can be promotional events, celebration events or events to support existing activities such as a school play. So the type of event could range from: a buffet served at an open evening, a formal sit down meal for guests at a prize-giving event, afternoon tea served at sports day or a pre-theatre supper served to the audience of the school or college musical.

Themes

An event can be made more interesting and fun by adding a theme. Below is a list of themes that could be considered.

Australian	English and St.George	Horror & Rocky Horror	Spanish
Autumn	Football	Horse Racing	Sports
Awards Night	French	Indian	St Patrick's
Balloons	German	Italian	Summer
Beach Party	Glow In The Dark	Mexican	Tropical
Black and White	Golf	Music	USA
Bollywood	Grand Prix	Nautical	Valentine
British	Greek	Oriental	Welsh
Casino	Halloween	Pirate	Wild West
Easter	Hen & Stag Night	School Days	Wimbledon
Mothers Day	Historical periods	Scottish	Wine

A film or television programme
Promoting local produce or organic, Fairtrade or one particular product, such as chocolate

There are specialist companies that provide a selection of products that help to create the theme.

The main considerations in all themed events are choosing the right food, drink, decorations and clothes to reflect the theme.

12.2 Investigating the task

As there are so many types of events, it is important to research possible events and then investigate possibilities and restrictions that the event suggests.

This section is worth 10 per cent or 5 per cent of the total 60 per cent or 30 per cent for the unit.

During the research and investigation, make sure you investigate:

- different themes and events – already discussed in Chapter 12.1
- venues and seating arrangements
- staffing possibilities and the different roles and responsibilities
- possible resources such as cost, equipment and time
- the types of dishes and menu that could be used
- the type of customer the event will cater for.

Venues and seating arrangements

It is very important early on in the investigation to find the right venue. Some events will require venues outside the college or school. Part of the investigation could be to visit venues and check the following:

1. Is it the right size for the type of event you are planning – how many people will it accommodate? Most venues will have maximum seating numbers for the different styles of seating, such as cabaret, boardroom and theatre style. Is it too small or too big?
2. How much does it cost to hire and what will be included? (for example, furniture)
3. Is it accessible, convenient and easy for guests to get to? Is there enough parking? Does it have facilities for people with special needs? (for example, a ramp for wheelchairs)
4. Are there suitable facilities for cooking and food storage?
5. Can you create the right ambience in the room for the event?

Staff roles and responsibilities

When planning an event, it is important to have enough skilled and competent staff for the different roles to meet the needs of the event. Members in a team will have different jobs and responsibilities. Also, working in a team will create a shared and balanced workload.

It is important that each member of the team is given a role that they are comfortable with. So part of the investigation could be to identify people's skills and attributes. Some people are happy to react with customers. Others prefer to work back-of-house and be involved in food preparation.

An industrial food mixer will allow for large quantities of cake or bread mixture to be produced so that a cake stall or pizza restaurant would be easy to run

Cost

At some stage in the investigation, a budget needs to be established. For all events, the organiser is given an amount of money to spend – a budget. This can be an overall budget or separated for different resources, such as food, drink and decorations. As part of the investigation, a list of resources that are likely to be needed could also be written.

Equipment

Every event needs a variety of equipment and materials. It is important to identify what equipment is available.

Once this has been identified, an investigation can be made into the availability and cost of other equipment and materials needed.

Time

At some stage, a date and time for the event needs to be decided. You must consider how much time you have to carry out all the work involved in planning for the event so that it is successful and every task is completed. Other timing considerations are:

- Does the event clash with any existing events?
- Is the venue available at that time?
- How long should the event run for?
- What is the time of day?
- What is the time of year – weather?

Dishes and menus

A large part of the investigation can be researching and trying out different dishes and menus. Analysing existing menus can help with decisions about the type and structure of the event menu. Trying out dishes in groups and tasting them helps considerably with decisions about what items to include. You need to use the practical skills learned throughout the course in this part of the investigation. For example: for a three-course meal the group could have four practical sessions where they try out starters, main course sauces, vegetables and desserts before they make a decision about the menu. See Chapter 7.6 for more information on menu planning.

Type of customer

It is important to consider the type of customer likely to attend different types of events but also consider the type of customer available for some events. For example, if a children's tea party is organised, will the children be at school when it is planned?

An industrial dishwasher saves time and allows for the serving and washing up of a five-course gourmet meal

ACTIVITY

Carry out a small activity where team members have to produce 100 quality biscuits but have not been given specific roles. Evaluate the activity to identify what roles each team member would be best at.

12.3 Planning the task

Careful planning means a successful event. This section is worth 7.5 or 3.75 per cent but is essential to the task.

Planning is all about applying the knowledge and understanding gained from the investigation and research to producing a plan of action for the event.

This detailed plan of action should include:
- how the event will be marketed
- the theme of the event and the presentation used to create the right ambience
- risk assessment chart
- a group and/or individual plan
- where the venue is and more details about the venue
- the dishes or menu being served
- costings for dishes and other items
- quantities of ingredients needed and the equipment required.

Marketing

Marketing is about communicating the event to customers. It is about raising people's awareness of the event and informing them about it. This can be done in several ways:

Advertising	Promotion	Personal selling
radio, newspapers, posters – billboards, leaflets, internet and other ways, such as bags, t–shirts, pens, and so on.	free samples, gifts, competitions, point-of-sale displays and demonstrations, free samples.	a very successful way of marketing.

Decisions need to be made about the marketing techniques to use. Think about which ones will be most effective, the cheapest and the least time consuming to do.

Theme and presentation

Themes and events have been discussed in Chapter 12.1. At the planning stage, the chosen idea can be fine-tuned so that the presentation methods are clear. For example, what type of napkin fold will be used, how will the table setting look and what will the staff wear?

Risk assessment

HACCP and risk assessments are discussed in detail in Chapter 3.9. Part of the planning process for any event is to carry out a detailed risk assessment so that all workers are clear about the possible areas of risk. An HACCP plan could also be produced if the event is in a different or unusual location, such as a village hall or the middle of a field.

Can you see the difference between good marketing technique and bad?

Adverts need to be informative and persuasive. They need to:
1 Catch attention.
2 Interest.
3 Create desire.
4 Cause action.

Group and individual plan

It is important that everyone carrying out the event knows what they should be doing at an exact time, as well as being aware of what other people should be doing. A detailed group plan does this.

An individual plan will give more detail about this timing for a particular person. For example a group plan will show a team member making desserts for three hours. An individual plan will break this down into the detail of production of three different desserts and the sequencing of these steps.

Venue

At the planning stage, the chosen venue also needs fine tuning with seating plans so that capacity is checked and confirmation or availability and timings are made.

Dishes and menu

The investigation of dishes and menus needs to be analysed at the planning stage so that decisions can be made about which to include in the final menu for the event.

This menu then needs to be communicated to customers before or during the events as some form of a menu card. It also needs to be used to inform group and individual planning as well as resource lists.

Costings

A total costing should be calculated that includes the following:
- hire of venue
- administration and promotional materials – flyers – posters
- stationery – invites and place cards
- food and drink
- payment for entertainment including technical equipment
- transport.

This should be within the overall budget given.

A detailed costing of individual dishes and the whole menu is also important. Some of this might be carried out at the investigation stage when dishes are being trialled, as decisions about suitable dishes to be used can be influenced by the cost of making them.

Quantities and equipment

A checklist of equipment needed for the event, whether it is available or needs to be hired, should be produced. Also, a list of all the materials needed, including a detailed ingredient list, should be produced. This is vital for the organisation of the event.

ACTIVITY

Use a room layout programme to plan out different room layouts for a specific event.

12.4 Carrying out the task

Thorough investigation and planning for an event should mean that it happens without any problems arising – that it is successful.

It is important that everyone involved in carrying out the event uses all the skills and knowledge they have learned throughout the course. This is because this section is worth 30 per cent or 15 per cent of the total GCSE mark.

It is important that you show excellent:

- personal presentation
- safe practices, including safe hygiene, showing consideration of risk assessment
- practical skills, including food and beverage preparation, production and service and customer care
- organisational skills, including time, choice and use of equipment and use of resources.

Self presentation is an important part of making a good impression

Personal presentation

This is very important whether you are front-of-house or backstage. Your clothes, hair and makeup are very important, especially backstage where hygiene is paramount, but personal presentation is also about your posture – 'how you hold yourself' and your manner – if you look welcoming and have a smile on your face. How you welcome customers can also be considered part of personal presentation. Backstage, how you react and work with others in the team could also be considered personal presentation.

Safe practices

This is about working hygienically and safely. It is about using the knowledge gained from learning about hygienic practices in Chapter 3 and possibly also from studying the Level 2 food safety exam. It is also about working safely – not leaving things out to trip over and being aware of fire risks (see Chapter 9.3). In summary it's about using the risk assessment carried out in the planning stage.

Practical skills

The event is where you can show off all the skills you have learned throughout the course. It is very important that you show as wide range of skills as possible and show the highest level of skill as possible.

Food and beverage preparation and production

You need to use all the food preparation skills learned in Chapters 7 and 8, as well as the food production skills learned in trial events. You need to show as many high-level skills, such as meat and fish preparation, use of complex sauces, pastry and bread-making, and high-level presentation skills as possible.

Food and beverage service and customer care

You need to use the food and beverage service skills learned in Chapter 9. When catering for an event, there are also special issues to consider such as:

- If it is buffet service, tables of customers need to be sent up to collect food one at a time or there will be long queues.
- It may be necessary to announce that food is being served – 'please be seated'.
- It is important to communicate with the chef if food needs to be delayed because of speeches or the entertainment.

Often customers have individual requests during the event. They might not like the food or drink being served, they might need a piece of equipment that isn't available or they might want you to tell them where things are. You need to remember that customer satisfaction is vital to the success of the event and that your customer service skills will be part of that success. You learned about customer service in Chapter 10.

> **EXAMINER'S TIP**
>
> You need to show initiative – identify what needs doing without being told to do it, for example, when plates need clearing or when a water jug needs filling or when a dish needs completing.

Organisational skills

It is very important that you are organised and work hard throughout the event. This includes clearing up after the event. It is important that you keep to the time plan so that you do not let the team down. Everyone needs to be able to do their share of the work if the event is to be successful. Practice events and development of practical skills throughout the course should help you to be as organised as possible.

You also need to be able to adapt to unexpected occurrences and even to be able to use contingency plans such as coping with accidents or emergencies, coping with staff shortages and changes to numbers of people attending.

12.5 Evaluating the task

Events are very rarely an absolute disaster but they are successful in varying degrees. It is important to evaluate this success so that suggestions can be made about how to improve subsequent events. This section of the task is worth 12.5 per cent or 6.25 per cent of the GCSE.

This section should include a detailed analysis and evaluation of the task and refer to all of the following areas:
- time management skills both before and during the event
- standards of personal hygiene
- safe and hygienic practices
- skills shown
- costing of dishes and the event
- customer satisfaction
- the success of the event
- improvements.

An evaluation of the task should always include a self-evaluation but also peer evaluations of team members. This should be done objectively – realistically, not subjectively – with personal comments.

Time management skills

If the group and individual plans are analysed, it will be easy to identify if everyone kept to their plan or if some people had too much or too little to do. It will be easy to identify whether some team members were not pulling their weight and whether some members said they could do far more than they were capable of. A self-evaluation of time management can also be done here.

Personal hygiene

Here a reflection of personal presentation and personal hygiene can be made. A read of Chapter 3.4 on personal hygiene would help this assessment.

Safe and hygienic practices

Personal hygiene isn't the only part of good hygienic practices. Methods of food storage, preparation and cooking are also important as well as cleaning and waste disposal. A read of Chapter 3.5 will help this evaluation as will a check of the risk assessment made during the planning of the task.

Skills

If you identify the skills you have used throughout the task, you can evaluate the range and level of skill that you have used. You can evaluate whether you have worked to the best of your ability.

Costing

This is about assessing the success of the event against the budget given and the expected profit that was made.

It is also about assessing how accurate the costing of dishes was against the actual cost and use of ingredients. A reflection on portion control could be included here.

A review of spending should have been made throughout the planning process. An evaluation of this review could also be made here.

Customer satisfaction

The customer is probably the most important person to get feedback from because they attended the event rather than ran it. If you do not give the customer an opportunity to feedback their opinions, you never really know if they are happy, satisfied or unhappy.

Customer feedback – asking customers if everything was satisfactory – can be formal or informal. See Chapter 10.2 for information.

Informal feedback	Formal feedback
You can get informal feedback by simply asking customers if they are having a good time of if everything is to their satisfaction, you can also get informal feedback by simply observing their behaviour.	Formal feedback can be gathered by a variety of means such as questionnaires, comment cards and internet or telephone surveys. A questionnaire can be written specifically for an event and a customer comment card would be a more general feedback form.

Formal feedback should be recorded and analysed, for example, by using an Excel spreadsheet.

The success of the event

This can be a summary evaluation of the event and answer the following questions:
- Did we charge the right price?
- Did we target the right customers?
- Did we include the right entertainment?
- Did we serve the right food and drink in the right quantities?
- Did we promote the event effectively?
- Did we hold the event at the right time at the right place?
- Did we make the right amount of profit?

So, were we successful?

Improvements

This final part of an evaluation is a reinforcement of the summary evaluation. For example, if it was felt that there was not enough choice of desserts, an improvement would say that more desserts would be offered next time. It would also suggest what type of dessert would be served especially if customer feedback said that there were not enough healthy choices.

13.1 Introduction to the controlled assessment

The controlled assessment is worth 60 per cent of the single award Catering GCSE and 30 per cent of the double award Hospitality and Catering GCSE. Because of this, it is very important to prepare for the two assessments, task 1 and task 2, to the best of your ability. It is important to understand how to achieve the best marks possible. To do this, you need to understand the structure of the assessments and the process you need to go through to enable you to get good marks.

There are three parts of the task for both assessments:
- planning the task
- carrying out the task
- evaluating the task.

What is the controlled assessment?

This is two practical tasks where you plan and then make a range of dishes. You then work out how successful you have been – you evaluate each task. The assessment tests you on your practical abilities. This is unlike the exam, which tests you on your theoretical knowledge of the industry. Carrying out the task counts for half of the marks. The other marks are for planning – research is part of this planning – and evaluating the task.

Because it is a large part of the final GCSE mark, it is important to practise these practical skills throughout the course so that the task is carried out at the highest ability level you have. It is also important to practice the planning and evaluating skills needed for the tasks.

KEY TERM

Commodity: food commodity is another term for ingredients. The term commodity is used when ingredients of the same type are grouped together, for example, meat, cereals, oils.

Task 1

This should be carried out by the end of Year 10. This task is based on commodities. It is worth 20 per cent of the single award Catering GCSE final mark and 10 per cent of the double award Hospitality and Catering GCSE final mark. The task should be chosen from one of the following:

1 Chefs use a wide range of fruit and vegetables to add colour, flavour and texture to their menus. Using fruit and vegetables, produce and serve four interesting dishes that would be popular with customers.	**2** There is a wide variety of dairy products available for a chef to use. Using dairy products, produce and serve two sweet and two savoury dishes that could be included on a menu.	**3** Rice and pasta are increasingly popular on restaurant menus as alternatives to potatoes. Using rice and pasta, produce and serve four colourful and interesting dishes that a chef could include on a restaurant menu.

All four dishes should be made at the same time. The suggested session time is approximately two hours.

Fifteen hours is allocated to the task and supporting written material showing planning and evaluation. This should be no more than eight A4-sized sheets.

Task 2

This task is carried out in Year 11. It is based on meal preparation where sequencing of cooking dishes becomes important. This task is worth 40 per cent of the single award Catering GCSE final mark and 20 per cent of the double award Hospitality and Catering GCSE final mark.

The task should be chosen from one of the following:

1 The local hotel in your area is holding an international week. As the trainee chef, you have been invited to take part and have been asked to prepare a two-course meal from a country of your choice.	**2** Celebrity chefs have been promoting the importance of a healthy diet. As a school/college caterer, you have been asked to produce and serve a two-course meal that would encourage healthy eating in the school/college restaurant.	**3** Vegetarian dishes should appear on every menu. While on work experience in a small hotel, you have been asked to produce and serve a two-course meal suitable for vegetarian guests. The dishes will then be included on the hotel's à la carte menu.

The suggested session time to produce this two-course meal is also approximately two hours.

Thirty hours is allocated to the task and supporting written material showing planning and the evaluation. This should be no more than twenty A4-sized sheets.

13.2 Investigating the task – what to investigate

Before the assessments are actually carried out, you need to find out more about the commodities or dishes that you think you will use. You need to think about all the different things you need to find out. You need to research and investigate all the different aspects.

Investigating task 1

This task is about commodities, either fruit and vegetables or dairy products or rice and pasta. To find out more about these, you need to consider:

Types available and ease of obtaining them

Each of the above commodities are very different. Fruit and vegetables are seasonal and there is a very wide range, as well as varieties of one particular fruit or vegetable. For example, tomatoes come in all shapes, sizes and flavours. Dairy products can be bought at any time of the year. Pasta and rice are grown and made in other countries. Some special-shaped pasta is difficult to find in main supermarkets and some rice is quite specialized, such as Camargue or black rice. You need to carry out research about the commodity you have chosen.

The cost of these ingredients

Cost is important and should influence the kind of dish you might make. Parmesan and Roquefort are very expensive cheeses and will increase the cost of a dish considerably. Most fruit and vegetables are cheap if they are bought in season. The cost of some fruit and vegetables can be a lot higher if they are flown in from around the world. Strawberries are a good example of this.

How to buy and store ingredients

Some commodities have a short shelf-life so the use-by date is important, as well as storing them in the fridge so that they do not cause food poisoning. Others have a long shelf-life but must be stored in a dry place. Some commodities need to be checked that they are not discoloured or bruised before buying them. Care needs to be taken in finding out about the buying and storing of all these foods.

Ingredients' uses and versatility and how easy they are to prepare

Once different types of commodities have been researched, it is important to learn about different recipes that can be used with them. How many different ways can these commodities be used? For example, sweet or savoury dishes, snacks, starters or main dishes. Working out how long it will take to prepare these recipes is also important.

The colour, flavour and texture of these ingredients

Only when recipes are researched can the above be considered. All dishes need a variety of colour, flavour and texture. It is important if you have a bland commodity such as rice that you work out how to add flavour. If a milk sauce is smooth, how do you add crunch to a dish using it?

The nutritive value

It is also worthwhile considering how balanced dishes are made with these commodities. Does the dish contain ingredients from more than one, and if possible nearly all, of the sections in the Eatwell plate?

Investigating task 2

All of the aspects mentioned above can also be considered for task 2. This task is about a two-course meal, which could be a starter and a main dish or a main dish and a sweet. Commodity investigation could be investigated further for this task so that you have a broader knowledge of commodities such as alternative proteins that vegetarians could eat.

The Eatwell plate

Use the Eatwell plate to help you get the balance right. It shows how much of what you eat should come from each food group.

Fruit and vegetables

Bread, rice, potatoes, pasta and other starchy foods

Meat, fish, eggs, beans and other non-dairy sources of protein

Foods and drinks high in fat and/or sugar

Milk and dairy foods

The government Eatwell plate

Other aspects to investigate could include:
- investigating the structure of a menu for a meal – analysing different menus
- how to present menus – analysing the presentation of existing menus
- how to present a meal – ways to layout and decorate food on a plate
- investigating table layouts and decorations – covered in Chapter 9.2.

Menu planning is covered in more detail in Chapter 7.6.

13.3 Investigating the task – how to investigate

It is important to understand that there are different ways to research and investigate and different ways to record the results of this work. Remember that all written supporting material for the task must be no more than eight A4 pages for task 1 and 20 A4 pages for task 2. This means that recording must be precise and concise.

Practical investigations

Not all research and investigation has to be reading and writing. Catering is a practical subject so research can be practical. Chefs spend time in their kitchens experimenting with ingredients and trying out new dishes or parts of dishes. They get their fellow workers to taste this trial food until everyone is happy with it. You can do the same thing. You can experiment with different ingredients and trial recipes to develop the best flavour and presentation. Trial recipes also help you with organisational skills. You will know how long each recipe takes to make and also the sequence in which you should make them. You can organise a tasting session with the people you work with or with some available adults, such as teachers. Make sure that you record the results of all your practical work so that you remember what you did and what people said. These results will help you to make decisions about your final dishes.

How to research

Chefs also go out and visit places to help them with ideas for ingredients and dishes. They will visit markets or supermarkets to look at available ingredients – at what is new or what looks fresh and in season. They will also go to different restaurants to try dishes and see how they could use some of the ideas they find in their own menus. Sometimes they will travel abroad to do this. You can visit your local market or supermarket or use the supermarket internet sites to find out what is available. You could also think about the restaurants you have visited or even arrange a special restaurant visit, such as one that specialises in vegetarian or Mexican food.

If your experience of ingredients and dishes is limited, ask other people about their experiences. You could write a questionnaire for adults to find out more about what ingredients or commodities they prefer and what kinds of dishes they choose when they eat in a restaurant.

It is important to use a variety of research techniques and not just rely on the internet or books at this stage. **It is also important to make sure that your research is not copying work taken directly from the internet or other sources of information.** This kind of research needs to be summarised in your own words. You need to explain what you have found out and learned from an internet search or from reading books and magazines.

Recording research

The quantity of supporting material is restricted but how that supporting material is presented is not. There is no reason why material other than A4 sheets cannot be submitted. You may feel that the best way to show your research, such as that of the types of available commodities, is to produce a leaflet, poster or display about them. Below are other suggestions:

Be imaginative in the way you record investigations, be concise and to the point.

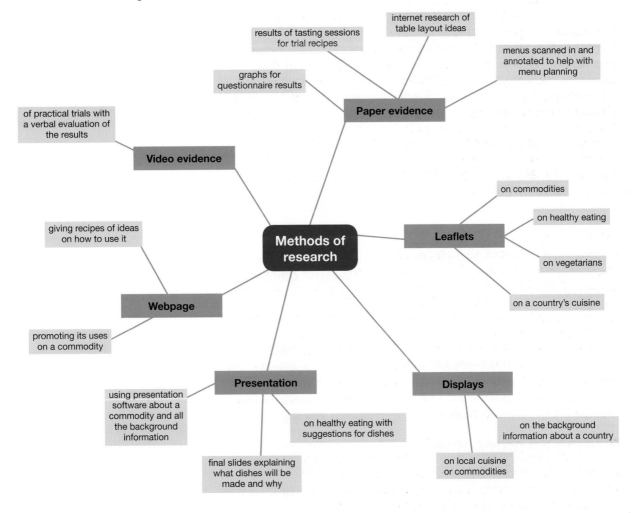

13.4 Planning for the task

Good planning allows you to be confident when you carry out the task. You know what you have to do and when you have to do it. You know why you have chosen your dishes and how you will present them. Planning involves:

- showing what dishes have been chosen – this could be as a written menu
- why the dishes have been chosen
- an order of work
- a shopping list for ingredients
- a list of extras required for the presentation of the dishes
- costings for the dishes
- how you will get feedback from the people trying your dishes
- the nutritional content of the dishes (task 2 only).

Justifying dishes chosen

The first part of the planning process is to state what dishes you have chosen. You then need to be able to explain why you have chosen them. This might be easier to do if you think about the following points:

1 Are they easy to make or did you choose them to show off your practical skills, for example, sauce-making or good chopping skills or bread-making.

2 Can you make the dishes in the time provided? You might have chosen one dish because it is quick to make, as the other dishes take some time to make.

3 Do you have the equipment to make them? You might have chosen one dish because you know there is a food processor available to help you prepare the dish quickly.

4 What colour, texture and flavours are all the dishes? Have you chosen a dish because it contrasts with other dishes in flavour or texture?

5 What is the cost of the ingredients? Have you chosen some dishes because they are inexpensive?

6 What is the nutritional content of the dishes? Even for task 1 you can comment on the general nutritional balance of the dishes. You can use the Eatwell plate to help you do this.

Writing an order of work

This is a very important part of planning as it guides you as you carry out the task.

This order of work should have clear instructions for each dish so that someone else could – if required – make the dishes.

That means that you cannot write: 'Make Bolognese sauce.'

You have to write the step-by-step process of making each dish.

For example: ' 1 Sweat onions for 10 minutes. 2 Add minced meat and brown.'

For task 1, the order of work will clearly show which dishes are being made first and which ones next, and so on.

For task 2, the order of work should show the correct sequence of making dishes and the dove tailing of tasks. This means that sometimes you might do part of the preparation for one dish and then part of another before the first dish is finished off. The correct sequencing of tasks is an important skill to learn and does need practice to develop confidence.

This order of work could also include control checks for steps that include safety – such as using oven gloves when taking hot trays out of the oven, hygiene – such as storing high-risk foods in the fridge until they are needed, or quality checks such as a visual check to see when a cake is cooked.

Don't take on too much at once in your planning!

KEY TERM

Sequencing: deciding the correct or best order to carry out a series of tasks.

TIME	TASK	CONTROL
12.10	Take the swiss roll out of the oven. Turn out of the tin, peel off the paper and leave to cool.	Use oven gloves. Check that the colour is golden brown and the cake springy.
12.15	Make the cheese sauce using the roux method: Melt the butter Add the flour and mix together. Cook gently for a few minutes, Take off the heat and very slowly add the milk – stirring all the time.	If lumps form use a hand whisk to get rid of them before you add any more milk.

Example of a task list

Shopping list for ingredients

Once you have chosen the dishes you will make, you need to collate all the ingredients from each recipe and write a complete list of ingredients required. This might be easier to read and then to shop for if ingredients are grouped under:

- fruit and vegetables – greengrocer
- meat and fish – butcher and fishmonger
- dairy products
- dried goods – flour, and so on.

13.5 Planning for the task – continued

Justifying the choice of dishes and showing how they will be made are the key parts of planning. To be totally successful at this stage, you also need to remember to carry out costings, how you get feedback from the tasting of the dishes, a plan for presentation (most important for task 2) and nutritional analysis (task 2).

Costing of dishes

Costing of dishes has been covered in Chapter 11.2.

For task 1, you need to calculate the portion cost for each dish you make. An easy way to do this is to use a special spreadsheet with formulas that will calculate the exact cost of each ingredient. There are several costing spreadsheets available on the internet. You can use a supermarket website to find out the cost of the ingredients you have used.

Total costs	£12.00
Cost after bulk-buying (÷4×3)	£9.00
Number of portions	6
Cost per portion	£1.50
Selling price (÷3×10)	£5.00

Calculating selling price

For task 2, you also need to calculate the selling price of the dishes or menu. Again, this has already been discussed in Chapter 11.2. Hospitality establishments work on around 30 per cent food costs so the cost needs to be divided by 3 and multiplied by 10. It is worthwhile remembering that establishments buy their ingredients in bulk and often get a discount in the price compared to supermarket prices. If you want to consider this when calculating costs, you could reduce the total cost of ingredients by a quarter to show this.

Feedback from tasting

It is worthwhile planning how you will record people's comments about your dishes so that when you evaluate the task you have information to use. It is worthwhile thinking about what you would like your dishes to turn out like. If you have practiced making them, you will have a clear idea. From this, you can pick out adjectives that describe the attributes of the dish. You can then ask the tasters to give each attribute marks out of five – five being excellent. You can set out a record sheet in a chart and if it helps with your evaluation, these results could be converted to attribute profiles using a spreadsheet.

There is a wide range of adjectives that can describe food by texture, appearance, taste, smell etc.

Presentation planning

This follows on from any research you have carried out on how dishes are presented and also how tables are set to create a good ambience for diners. This planning is likely to be relevant for task 2, when you are producing a meal not just a range of dishes. This planning might be in the form of a list of extras you will need such as:

- napkins
- tablecloth
- glasses
- cutlery
- crockery
- flowers and vase
- candle.

The list could also include a menu that you have or will design using a desk-top publishing package or one you have written by hand.

Another way to show this planning is to draw a bird's-eye view of the table settings, labelling and explaining each item.

Nutritional analysis

There are several IT programs that analyse the nutritional content of dishes and meals. When using these programs, it is important to analyse a portion rather than a recipe to get a correct analysis of what a dish provides towards daily recommended amounts of nutrients. To do this, the quantities of each ingredient needs to be reduced. For example, a recipe that is for four people will need the ingredients quartered. The IT program might not explain whether a dish has a good nutritional balance or not. If a dish provides 200 per cent of the recommended daily amount of Vitamin C, this is alright as Vitamin C helps protect against infections. But, if a dish provides 200 per cent of the recommended daily amount of sodium, this is not good as a high salt diet (sodium chloride is salt) can cause high blood pressure and lead to strokes and death. You need a thorough knowledge of nutrition and healthy eating to analyse dishes successfully.

Texture and feel	Appearance	Taste and smell
brittle	appealing	acid
chewy	attractive	bitter
cold	clear	bland
crisp	colourful	burnt
crumbly	crumbly	creamy
crunchy	dry	dry
dry	fattening	fatty
flaky	fresh	old
gooey	greasy	salty
greasy	healthy	sharp
gritty	hot	sickly
hot	moist	soggy
juicy	smooth	sour
lumpy	soggy	spicy
mushy	tasty	stale
powdery		sweet
rubbery		watery
slimy		tangy
smooth		tasteless
springy		tasty
sticky		undercooked
stringy		
tender		
tough		
watery		
warm		

13.6 Carrying out the task

Preparing, cooking and serving the dishes in both tasks accounts for 30 per cent (single Catering GCSE) or 15 per cent (double Hospitality and Catering GCSE) of the final GCSE mark. It is important that you carry out these tasks to the best of your ability to achieve the highest marks possible. These tasks allow you to apply all the knowledge and skills you have learned throughout the GCSE course.

You need to demonstrate:

- high standards of personal hygiene
- high standards of kitchen hygiene
- the safe use of equipment and working safely
- good technical skills and a wide variety of these skills
- organised and independent work, which for task 2 would show good sequencing and dovetailing of tasks
- high standards of final presentation.

A collection of the foods you can use for the task

Personal hygiene

Correct procedures for personal and food hygiene have all been covered in Chapter 3. To recap some points, it is suggested you wear the correct clothing and that this includes a hat. You shouldn't wear any jewellery or nail varnish and your hair should be tied back. Wash your hands regularly, especially after handling raw meat and dealing with rubbish. You need to show good personal habits, such as no coughing over food and no scratching of ears or nose. You also need to taste your food and test for seasoning in the correct way. This is with a clean spoon that is then washed up.

Food hygiene

Again, this has been covered in Chapter 3. It is important that you show a high level of understanding of food hygiene. This includes storage of ingredients, preparation and cooking rules and also cleaning.

You must store high-risk foods, such as milk and chicken in a fridge until it is needed and make sure that dishes made from these types of food are not left out in the danger zone for any longer than an hour and a half.

You must make sure that all preparation equipment is clean and that it is cleaned again after the preparation of raw meat or poultry. A 'clear and clean as you go' system needs to be followed as this means everything will remain clean but also safe. You must allow time for this cleaning in your order of work.

Following correct cooking procedures is also important. You can check that high-risk foods are cooked correctly by using a temperature probe. The temperature must be 75°C for 15 seconds.

Working safely

High standards of hygiene also allow good levels of safety. For example, if a work area is kept clean and tidy with ingredients being put back into the fridge and washing up done regularly, this also helps with safety. You are less likely to fall because of spillages or cut yourself on a hidden knife. Correct use of sharp knifes is a key safety skill – choosing the right knife for the job and cutting ingredients with the right hand-holds is important. It is also important to use a cooker safely – no pan handles towards the front and using oven gloves – not a tea towel.

It is important to check the temperature of food being cooked; along with many other safety issues

Use of equipment

Using equipment saves time. Using equipment shows off good technical skills because it shows that you can recognise when equipment is useful, for example, using an electric whisk to whisk egg white or using a food processor to grate a large quantity of cheese instead of a hand grater. You must be able to use this equipment safely and then be able to clean it safely as many pieces have sharp blades. You must also be able to show that you understand the danger of electricity around water and the importance of turning this equipment off after it has been used.

All of the above points mentioned may have been highlighted as control checks in the order of work. If they have, the order of work will remind you about working safely and hygienically.

13.7 Carrying out the task – continued

The most important skills to demonstrate during each task are the technical skills you have learned during the course. You want to be able to show how well you can prepare, cook and serve food.

Technical skills

Chopping up fruit for a fruit salad is a technical skill. Chopping up an orange in a professional way so that there is no pith left on the segments shows a higher level of skill. Spinning caramel for presentation or boning a mackerel are also high-level skills.

Below is a list of some of the skills you might use. They are divided into basic, medium and high levels of skill. You must try to include as many skills as possible in your task. These should be as many high-level skills as possible and as wide a range of skills as possible.

Basic skills	Medium-level skills	High-level skills
• Assembling of ready-made components such as pizza base, sauce, etc., trifle made from sponge fingers, fruit and a carton of custard or sausage rolls using puff pastry • scones • crumbles • creaming method for cakes • salads, such as tuna and pasta salad	• bread-making, including for pizzas • whisking method for cake making • shortcrust pastry • basic sauce-making, such as all-in-one and tomato sauce • presentation of simple starters with good presentation skills such as melon or garlic mushrooms • soups • preparation of simple starters • stir-fry or rissotto	• bread-making where flavour, finish and shape have been developed • flaky or rough puff pastry • roux method of sauce-making and other skilled sauces, such as reductions • meat and fish preparation • use of gelatine for desserts such as mousses • development of a Swiss roll to a roulade • sequencing of different cooking times such as a mixed grill

Organised and independent work

It is important to understand when to ask for help if you have forgotten how to do something or you have made a mistake and don't know how to sort it out. But it is important to try to remember for yourself and try to work out what to do. You must try to work as independently as possible if you want to gain good marks. Over the course, you will have developed your skills in working independently and also had practice making the kind of dishes required for the task. Having a good order of work to follow will help you with your organisational skills, as will allowing yourself enough time for preparation at the beginning of the task.

Good sequencing and dovetailing of tasks (task 2)

Some people think cooking a traditional roast dinner is easy. You put the meat and potatoes in the oven, you boil a few vegetables and it's all cooked an hour or so later. Actually, being able to get the meat, potatoes, carrots and cabbage as well as the gravy and possibly Yorkshire puddings ready all at the same time is challenging and requires good sequencing of tasks.

If you are making a two-course meal, you need to have the first course – whether it is the main or starter – ready first and then the next course. You need vegetables or any other accompaniments ready at the same time as the main part of the dish. This usually requires you to prepare parts of dishes at different times. For example, if you are making a trifle and chicken cordon bleu with dauphinoise potatoes, braised cabbage and julienne carrots, you will probably follow this sequence:

1 Make the Swiss roll.
2 Make the real custard.
3 Let these cool down.
4 Prepare the potatoes and cabbage and leave them cooking.
5 Assemble the trifle and put it in the fridge.
6 Prepare the cordon bleu.
7 Chop and slice the carrots, then cook them.
8 Cook the cordon bleu.
9 Serve.

High standards of final presentation

All dishes need to look nice if you want people to enjoy them. This is particularly important for meals served in a restaurant. Garnishes can be added and care taken in how you place all the component parts of the dish. You must give yourself time to finish off all your dishes so that you do not miss out on marks. Correct portion size is part of presentation. You do not want to overwhelm customers with an enormous portion or disappoint them with a tiny portion.

13.8 Evaluating the controlled assignment

Evaluating each task once it has been carried out is important and carries separate marks (5 per cent and 7.5 per cent). Evaluations need to cover several points in detail. In order to make sure that your evaluation is detailed and covers all the relevant points, it is suggested that you use a relevant writing frame or at least use the headings below to advise you. Each heading should be a paragraph long.

Suitability of dishes

This is the introduction to the evaluation and is where you can justify your choice of dishes for the task. Once you have made the dishes, you will have a clear idea of how successful they have been. For example, were they healthy or suitable for a vegetarian or were the fruit and vegetable dishes interesting.

Time management

Sometimes in a restaurant, you have to wait ages for your meal to be served. This is often because of poor time management. You need to comment on your own time management: if you took too long over certain tasks or if you did not choose your dishes wisely and actually had time to spare. You might have been just right and completed your task on time. An explanation on why you think this happened is a good idea, such as the fact that you practiced making the dishes several times.

Using a writing frame helps you gain good marks in this section. It helps to make sure you have covered all the areas required in an evaluation

---

Suitability of dishes

I have chosen to make _____ because I thought _____ and it _____.

Time management

When I carried out the task, I thought I managed my time _____ because I _____ and _____.

I thought I should have _____ and _____

Customer acceptance

Feedback from my customers/tasters was _____. They said that the appearance of _____ dish was _____ and I thought _____. The taste was _____ and the texture was _____. They said _____.

Suggestions for improvements

If I did this task again I would change _____ and not do _____ because _____.

Costings and portion control

The cost of a portion of _____ is _____ which I think is _____.

Therefore, the selling price would be _____ which is _____.

The portion sizes were _____ which is _____.

Nutritional content (task 2 only)

When I analysed the nutritional content, I found out that _____ which is _____.

So I could _____ to improve _____.

I _____ this task and learned _____ from it.

Customer acceptance

If the customer – whoever has tasted the dishes – has been asked to fill in an evaluation sheet, this part of the evaluation will be made easier. If others have made comments on the appearance, taste and texture of each dish, you can summarise their, and also your own, opinions in the evaluation. This section can be quite detailed as what the actual dishes turned out to be like is the focus of this evaluation.

Suggestions for improvements

'Virtually no dish is perfect, there is always some little thing that can be improved' said a Michelin-starred restaurant chef. So there is likely to be something to comment on for this section. For example, if you felt that one of your dishes wasn't very colourful, then you could suggest that if you made it again you would make it more colourful and suggest how you would do so. You could suggest: adding a variety of vegetables including orange carrots, green peas and red pepper.

Costings and portion control

In task 1, comment on the cost per portion for each dish you have made and whether you think any dish was expensive or cheap. You could highlight some of the expensive ingredients used and suggest ways to reduce the cost of some dishes.

In task 2, this evaluation needs to be more detailed and you need to comment on the likely selling price of each dish on the menu. This is easy to do if you compare how much a portion would cost in a restaurant or a supermarket. Part of this calculation is working out the portion size of the dishes and making sure that they are a suitable size for an average person. You also need to comment on the profitability of the dish.

Nutritional content (task 2 only)

In task 2, as part of the planning process, the nutritional content of each dish has been calculated. In the evaluation, this content needs to be discussed and analysed. To do this, you need a good understanding of healthy eating and the nutrients that make up foods. You need to know what nutrients we need a lot of and why we need them. You also need to know what nutrients we often eat too much of and why we should not have too much of them. With this knowledge, you can analyse the content of the dishes easily and also discuss ways to improve this nutritional content. For example, if a dish is high in salt that can cause high blood pressure, you can suggest other ways to season the dish, such as adding herbs or garlic.

Finishing an evaluation

A final sentence at the end of the evaluation is always a good idea even if it just says: 'I enjoyed this task and learned a lot from it.'

Index

Page numbers in **bold** type refer to key terms